CW00494400

Beer Brewing Bliss: Extract Brewing Basics

How To Brew Award-Winning Beer at Home Without The Fuss

Miles Goodman

Contents

A Special Gift to My Readers

As a thank you for purchasing this book, I have included a **FREE discount code document** containing amazing discounts from the above retailers.

The very best brewing equipment doesn't come cheap, so I'm sure you'll find this document of value as you begin your journey.

Visit my website and let me know where to send your copy of this incredible offer.

www.beerbrewingbliss.com

Introduction

Welcome aboard the good ship, beer.

As a passion of mine for many years, I felt it time to part with the knowledge and wisdom I've gained from carrying out this seemingly complicated process and condensing it into something manageable. The internet is flooded with contradictory information (and not just about beer making); it can be challenging to know which information to trust and which to banish to the pits of hell.

This simple book takes what looks like a dystopian nightmare and turns it into a simple process that can be followed by even those who know very little or even nothing about homebrewing.

Having purchased this book, you may already have many questions about the process: particularly the difficulty, cost, and amount of time that should be invested to achieve outstanding results. Unfortunately, there are no simple answers to these questions, and it really does depend on how much of each of these things you have or are willing to part with. However, whatever you decide, I'm confident that you'll find brewing somewhat of a liberating hobby. Who needs the pub when you're that good, right?!

As you may already be aware, you may follow two main methods when brewing beer at home: extract brewing and all-grain brewing. This book will focus solely on the former, ensuring that you know exactly which equipment you need and the most important things to consider at each stage. For those keen to learn about the biochemistry of fermentation, I have even thrown in some rather complex science at no extra cost. After all, science is a big part of my day-to-day life, and I'd be lost without it.

All-grain brewing is very different from extract brewing, at least for the first part of the brewing process. In the name of simplicity and steady progress, I have written a completely different book, *Beer Brewing Bliss: All-grain Brewing Mastery*, which addresses the more complex principles of all-grain brewing. This is like a sequel, akin to 'Empire Strikes Back', only better. (Yeah, right, Miles?!)

The two books in this series are like conjoined twins, and I would not recommend reading one without the other. Indeed, do not read the second book before completing this one; you will miss some vital information. You may also be asked to refer back to this book for a refresher course at specific points in the second book.

After completing the series, you should be endowed with all the information you need relating to equipment needs, cost, sanitisation, water management, malting, mashing, wort boiling, wort cooling, yeast pitching, fermentation, lagering, and everything in between. But don't panic: when you walk up a flight of stairs, you usually do so one step at a time, which is the philosophy I have used to guide you through the beer brewing process.

At this stage, I won't begin to talk about the ingredients needed for beer or the process itself, as that would spoil all the fun later. Instead, these opening paragraphs serve merely to set the scene for what will hopefully be a relatively smooth journey from novice to all-grain brewing master.

It is, however, essential to know the magical nature of what you are undertaking.

Beer is something that has been enjoyed by people for millennia and has a rich history dating back to ancient Persia, Mesopotamia, and Egypt. The first recorded history of beer brewing using barley was as far back as 5,000 BC. However, some sources point to even older brews carried out by the ancient Sumerians up to 8,000 years ago. Regardless of beer's exact time of origin, we should thank the Lord that humans have been practising the art of brewing for so long, thus allowing us to enjoy the sensational brews we are now accustomed to.

Of course, brewing was not as scientific back then as it is today, nor was beer produced on a larger commercial scale using complex measuring devices. As far as we know, it wasn't until the 7th century AD that beer was produced commercially by monasteries across medieval Europe. Although commercial, brewing was still more an art than a science, given the absence of equipment such as thermometers and hydrometers. The industrialisation of beer making finally came during the industrial revolution of the 19th century, when domestic beer making had sadly begun to diminish.

Today, the beer industry spans from small independent craft breweries to multinational companies, which share sales of over 133 billion litres per year (35 billion gallons) and about $300 billion in revenue. In recent years, mainly due to the introduction of mind-numbing 'stay at home' orders, I'm glad to say that domestic beer brewing has seen somewhat of a resurgence. At least we don't get viruses by staying at home brewing beer (unless our equipment is not correctly sanitised). All the more, the reason to enjoy the process—and more importantly, the end product.

Finally, the most blissful aspect of brewing, bar none, is the ability to share your creation with friends and even build new friendships on your journey down the rabbit hole. You can invite friends to help, watch, dance, or even drink your last batch as you brew. Brewing truly has the capacity to light up life during dark times.

So, without further ado, let's begin...

Chapter One

Home Brewing Kits

Before diving into the ins and outs of home brewing kits, it is first necessary to say a few things about extract brewing: what it is and how it is different from all-grain brewing.

A malt extract is boiled with hops in extract brewing to form the wort (pronounced 'wert') or unfermented beer. Malt extract is made commercially by extracting the fermentable sugars from selected barley grains and making them into a concentrate. They can be made either wet or dry, only differing by water content (usually 20% for liquid malt extract, LME, and almost none for dry malt extract, DME). Liquid and dry malts of the same kind contain an identical fermentable sugar profile. However, it is essential to note that these cannot be used like-for-like due to the concentration of sugar being lower in liquid malt extract than in DME. Hopefully, your high school science class will help you understand this concept, but if not, don't worry—the instructions will guide you.

There are three main advantages to using a malt extract to make your wort, the first and most important being the small investment. Suppose you aren't sure whether brewing will be for you or you haven't entirely made it to the end of the month with a dime to spare. In that case, malt extract is a great way to assess whether you enjoy the process and want to save for more expensive equipment next time around.

Homebrew starter kits are relatively inexpensive and can be purchased online for as little as $50 (£36). That is for a standard kit with two fermentation buckets, siphon, thermometer, hydrometer, stirring paddle, spigot tap, sanitiser, and airlock. After a quick internet search in the UK, the companies that offer the best deals on home brewing starter kits include Love Brewing, Bigger Jugs, Brew2Bottle, and Young's. I'm sure there is just as good a selection wherever you reside—unless you live in rural Antarctica. The companies mentioned are also reasonably priced for equipment if you want to buy items separately, which I will discuss in the next chapter. After purchasing your starter kit, you will have to buy the beer ingredients, as these are generally not included. Your homebrew starter kit can then be used repeatedly with different recipe packs.

The second advantage of using a home brewing starter kit is less room for error. One of the main worries novice homebrewers have is whether their brew will turn out drinkable. Nobody wants to wait with bated breath for three weeks to find that their brew tastes like, well, whatever disgusting word you'd like to use... So, using a pre-packaged malt extract containing the correct fermentable sugar profile will definitely set you off on the right foot.

Sure, there are still some mistakes you could make, like adding the wrong quantity of water or yeast or not sanitising correctly—however, the chances of making errors are significantly reduced with kits as most things are measured out for you, and clear instructions are always given. In addition, malt extracts are produced professionally. The sugar profile is of quality and will consistently deliver the desired taste.

The final advantage is time. Like sex, this is something that nobody ever has enough of—unless, of course, you're making homebrew that instantly makes the opposite sex fall at your feet. (And no, I don't mean by making it so strong that they can no longer stand.) Using a malt extract reduces the time significantly on brew day. You don't need to mash the grain, sparge, and lauter (words you will become familiar with in all-grain brewing mastery). Instead, you will add your malt extract to boiling water and begin brewing, adding the necessary hops as advised.

In contrast, there are some disadvantages to the extract brew method: the main one being the lack of creative control. When it comes to designing and/or changing the grain profile of your beer, you are very limited by the types of malt extract available. When using grains in the all-grain process, you can be much more selective over the flavours you give the wort and the flavour balance of the final product. Think of it like this: when making a doughnut, you can add as many toppings as you like (representing the hops), but the final product is only ever as good as the dough used at the beginning (representing the malt).

Finally, malt extracts can become expensive, mainly if you mix different types or if the recipe calls for a larger quantity. It is much cheaper to buy the grain itself for the all-grain brewer. But then, much like having a chauffeur, you're paying for the privilege of not having to take the time to do the leg-work yourself. Time is money, after all.

Chapter Two

Buying Equipment Separately

Take a tour of a craft brewery, and you'll find it looks very much like brewing is a major industrial pursuit. Even a local brewer with no distribution footprint has lots of hardware: steaming mash tuns, fermentation tanks, and numerous canning lines. Production staff will wander about wearing rubber boots, gloves, and aprons, hoisting grain bags and brandishing huge wooden paddles. It all looks costly, but the comforting news is that it takes years to build up to this level, so you won't be contacting your mortgage advisor or having any awkward discussions with the bank just to make a few batches of homebrew. In truth, you don't need to spend much money on fancy brewing equipment.

With that being said, if you do have a little extra cash left in your budget after buying your home brewing kit, you might want to invest in some higher-quality equipment for your second batch.

Brewer-specific equipment purchased separately will make your homemade beer's measuring, boiling, cooling, racking, fermenting, and packaging much more effortless. It will reduce the mess in the kitchen, lower the chance of spoiled beer, and save you a few logistical headaches (not to mention those from your partner).

Finally, any quality hardware you buy will often last you a lifetime of brewing. So, let's take the time to explore the options available.

Brew Pots

We've all walked away from a pot of boiling pasta and came back to find the stove flaming up and our kitchen full of steam. Boil-overs happen all the time in cooking, but only homebrewers know of the mental pain of an insufficiently-sized brewing pot spilling over and coating the stove and floor in wort. This is terrible news for both you and your beer. It reduces the amount you make and covers your kitchen in burnt-molasses residue that you then have to clean.

With this in mind, it's hardly any wonder why one of the first extra purchases made by the enthusiastic homebrewer is a large pot or brewing kettle.

Pots and Kettles - Brew pots come in a range of sizes from two-gallons all the way up to ten-gallons. Because most brewing kits contain five-gallon recipes, that measure should be your minimum pot size. Brew pots have an advantage over run-of-the-mill cooking pots because they are explicitly designed for wort production. A good brewing pot maintains a diameter-to-height ratio that will optimise heat distribution. It will also be designed to minimise scorching, which is critical when pouring in the viscous, sugary syrup.

A brew pot is your most affordable option for grain steeping and wort boiling. Even a high-end five-gallon pot will cost less than $50 (£36). A middle-of-the-road option from a reputable manufacturer might cost as little as $20 (£14). Running a quick search online is usually a good starting point to find the best deal for your budget.

However, if you want to spend a bit more on your boil, many suitable brew kettles are available on the market. A kettle differs from a pot in that it has a spigot tap to aid wort transfer.

A higher-end brew kettle may also have some of the following features:

- A steel ball valve to regulate the flow of liquid during transfer
- A dip tube on the interior to catch wort that rests below the spigot
- A vertical sight glass so you can check your evaporation loss in real-time
- A built-in thermometer
- Thermostat and heating element

While none of these is integral to your process, they can be magnificent savers of time and labour, ultimately making the brewing experience a little sweeter.

Brew kettles are moderately more expensive than pots. A kettle sporting most of the mentioned features will likely cost you around $100 (£70). However, a self-heating kettle will likely cost at least twice this amount due to its own built-in thermostat and heating element.

One often-overlooked advantage of pots and brew kettles is that they tend to have clear gallon markings etched on the inside. This makes light work of measuring out your brewing water and reduces the chance of error.

Hob Kettles vs Electric Kettles - This brings us to the question: should you stick with a stovetop brew kettle. Or should you dish out the extra cash for a self-heating electric model? You can get most of the 'bells and whistles' listed in either form. If you decide on the hob model, you might end up saving two hundred dollars, which could buy you a lot of malt and hops!

In contrast, the value of an electric brew kettle can be summed up in two words: control and mobility.

While you might have a powerful heat source on your gas stove, it can be challenging to hone in on the ideal temperature. Steeping malts at too high or too low a temperature will adversely impact your final product. A quality thermostatically-controlled electric kettle allows you to select the correct temperature on the kettle itself and maintain it.

In terms of mobility, the main advantage of having an electric brew kettle is that it liberates you from the kitchen. You can brew wherever there's a power source. Believe me: nothing beats being able to spread out on a warm afternoon and brew up some wort under a clear blue sky. That in itself might be worth the additional cost.

Electric kettles are also marginally more energy efficient and tend to heat faster; however, they won't produce the same rolling boil as a stove-heated kettle.

Aluminium vs Steel - When choosing the brew pot or kettle right for you, you should also consider what it's made from. All products on the market are made from either aluminium or stainless steel. It all comes down to how much cash you want to dish out upfront and how much maintenance and cleaning you're willing to do later.

Let's consider the pros and cons of each material:

- **Stainless Steel** is much stronger and more durable than aluminium. It is also less likely to leech off-flavours into the wort and is easier to clean. In contrast, steel heats up slower than aluminium and is usually more expensive.
- **Aluminium** is more affordable than stainless steel. It is often lighter and easier on your back when transporting large volumes of wort. It also heats up quicker. In contrast, aluminium is more prone to abrasions. It will need to be more fastidiously cleaned to protect its oxide layer. This prevents impurities from transferring to the wort during the brew.

Choosing Your Pot or Kettle - This may seem like a lot of information. Still, it's definitely worth taking the time to carefully consider which is the best type of vessel for your brew. Even if you're starting with a small pre-portioned recipe kit, you will want to have a pot or kettle that can handle both stress and volume. It should hold at least five gallons of water and be strong enough not to crack after a couple of batches.

You don't have to purchase all your equipment at once. If you only have limited funds, it's always best to ensure that you have the right-sized container from a well-regarded manufacturer, such as Blichmann or others. Over time, you can always augment your no-frills pot with some additional equipment.

Brewing Utensils

First-time homebrewers often forget one essential tool until they start to make their first batch of wort—and not just an everyday item will do. I'm talking about the brewing spoon or paddle. Don't forget to have one of these to hand, ready to mix in your malt extract, stir in the hops, and fish out any spent ingredients before fermentation.

In terms of quality, you want something durable and safe, capable of handling high temperatures and heavy/wet ingredients. It should also be slotted to sieve off any excess wort. The spoon/paddle types available are as follows:

- **Wooden Spoons** - Although there's something nostalgic about using an old wooden spoon, unfortunately, they aren't ideal for home brewing. They crack easily at high temperatures. Their porous nature means that they catch many bacteria that can negatively affect future brews.
- **Plastic Spoons** - A plastic stirring spoon or paddle is better. It's easy to clean and won't scrape your brew pot. Just make sure that the plastic is graded for food use and can withstand high temperatures.
- **Stainless Steel Spoons** - This is your best option for a brewing spoon or paddle. Stainless steel is dense and robust. It doesn't catch many rogue microbes (if any), making it easy to clean and sterilise. Just be careful not to scratch your new pot or kettle whilst stirring.

Like everything in this world, brewing spoons and paddles vary significantly in price but are generally inexpensive. The most expensive stainless steel paddles will cost you around $25 (under £20). This is a worthwhile investment, and if you get a good one, it will last you for years. You don't want anything to cause a 'stir' on brew day!

Fermentation Buckets & Carboys

One more piece of good news is that you don't need a massive fermentation tank to convert your wort into fantastic beer. In fact, you can create a stellar brew in a five-gallon plastic bucket. This may be the best option for someone just starting out, due mainly to the low cost.

However, the keener novice brewer may want to purchase the fancier glass carboy, also known as a demijohn. These fermentation vessels look like tankards that sit on top of office water coolers. In fact, using one of these empty tankards is another excellent option for fermentation. If you're really sneaky, you may even be able to steal a full one from the office store cupboard and use the water. Although, don't be leaving anyone in the office dehydrated.

Buckets and carboys have their own very long list of pros and cons, which I will now explore:

Function - To be clear, both buckets and carboys serve precisely the same function: providing a sheltered, sterile place for yeast to work on the sugars in your wort. Over the centuries, beer has been fermented in clay jars, wood casks, vessels left open in the ground, and super-sterile steel tanks. If you treat your bucket or carboy well, it will serve its purpose with distinction.

Affordability - Buckets win this one hands-down. You can find a perfect 6.5-gallon bucket with an airtight lid for $10-$20 (£15). If you're just starting as a homebrewer, this is all you need. A glass carboy of similar size, on the other hand, will cost you closer to $40-$50 (£30). Of course, when you're thinking about cost, you also need to consider the following:

Longevity - Buckets have a far shorter lifespan than glass carboys because plastic can only take so much punishment before scratches and gouges appear. These abrasions are more than just unsightly; they're little traps for bacteria to grow. So, you should always be proactive in replacing fermentation buckets. You don't want your plastic expiration warning to be a bad batch of beer.

Air Space - When yeast eats away at the fermentable sugars in the wort, it doesn't just produce ethanol. It also releases carbon dioxide bubbles. Hence, your fermentation vessel should leave ample room for this gas to disperse and a pathway for it to escape. At the same time, your fermenter needs to be airtight to prevent contamination.

Each fermentation option accomplishes this balancing act differently. Fermentation buckets leave plenty of empty space above the wort. They usually come with an airtight seal and a hole at the top for an airlock. Carboys are more compact, leaving less air above the wort. Although they only have a narrow opening through which carbon dioxide can escape, this opening can be filled with stoppers, bungs, or caps.

So, which option provides better air regulation for your burbling, foaming wort? Here is a breakdown of the pros and cons relating to airflow specifically:

- **Plastic buckets** provide plenty of headroom for gas to accumulate, and their lids usually are airtight by design. In contrast, more empty space in the bucket increases the chance of oxidation. Also, to check on fermentation progress, you need to open the bucket, further increasing the oxidation risk.
- **Carboys** are smaller, allowing for less air, thus reducing oxidation risk. Tapered neck funnels also direct oxygen straight out the top of the vessel. The clear glass means you can monitor fermentation without opening the carboy. The only drawback is making sure the stopper, bung, or cap is tight enough.

All things considered, a glass carboy does provide better air regulation. As much of the quality of a beer relies on air space and flow, this factor alone might be the decider for the more dedicated homebrewer.

Mobility and Storage - Don't overlook the importance of having a fermenter that you can move and store easily. Most fermentation yeast requires a cool, dark location, and that's typically not the exact spot that you conducted the wort boil. So, any fermentation vessel must be transported to a suitable location and potentially moved again for either secondary fermentation or bottling.

All fermenting vessels are awkward to carry because they contain gallons of heavy wort. However, you'll want to minimise sloshing, which oxidises your liquid.

Plastic is lighter than glass, and many fermentation buckets come with handles for ease of transport. Glass carboys, on the other hand, are much heavier and difficult to grip with bare hands. You can 'get a grip' on this problem by purchasing a $10 neck handle for your carboy or simply wearing thick gloves like those used for gardening.

Cleaning and Sanitising - In 2015, Chicago's Goose Island Brewing famously issued thousands of refunds after its coveted Bourbon County Stout series fell victim to an infection caused by *Lactobacillus acetotolerans* somewhere along the fermentation and packaging process. Chicago Tribune beer writer Joel Noel memorably described one of the infected stouts—which generally have a whiskey-soaked fudge brownie character—this way:

"It's like metallic pepper spent a year at the bottom of a garbage can in a sweaty gym sock and, well, just don't drink it" (Noel 2016).

The moral of the story is that you need to keep your fermentation equipment sterile.

Buckets also take the lead over carboys when considering the ease of cleaning. Their wide-open, un-tapered design makes scrubbing, rinsing, and sterilising easy. On the other hand, Carboys are bulkier, unyielding, and have a tiny opening. Post-fermentation goo and crust can be tough to remove, and you'll definitely need to purchase a few curved brushes. You'll also have to fill and empty the container multiple times during cleaning. If you're feeling particularly lazy, carboy-cleaning attachments are available for your power drill. Still, these will add another \$20-\$30 (£20) to your costs.

Bear in mind that while fermenter buckets are easier to clean, they are also more prone to catching unseen agents inside scratches or abrasions. This is a problem you don't have with glass carboys.

So, which Fermenter is Right for You?

To recap on the above points:

- Both fermenter buckets and glass carboys will serve all necessary functions for converting wort into beer.
- Plastic buckets are significantly less expensive than carboys.
- Glass carboys have a much longer lifespan than plastic buckets.
- Glass carboys are better designed for air regulation during the fermenting phase.
- Plastic buckets are, on average, lighter weight and easier to transport than carboys.
- Plastic buckets are much easier to clean and sterilise than carboys. Still, they are prone to minor damage that can lead to bacterial accumulation.

With all of these variables taken into account, you may wonder, “Is there a definitive best option”?! While I can’t state categorically that either a bucket or carboy is better overall, I would say that one is definitely better for the beginning homebrewer: a simple fermenting bucket is user-friendly, malleable, transportable, and inexpensive. After a few batches, it will be time to replace the bucket, and then you can decide whether you want to stick or twist.

Plastic Carboys - The previous carboy discussion focused solely on glass products; however, there are plastic carboys available. These products are lighter than glass, clocking in at about a quarter of the weight. They usually are cheaper, too: rarely more than $30 (£20) for a five-gallon size.

Plastic carboys have many of the same benefits as their glass counterparts. They are transparent, allowing for careful observation, and they have a tapered design for optimal oxygen dispersal. Alas, they also have the same disadvantages as glass carboys when it comes to storage and cleaning. Their plastic composition has the same damage risks and short lifespan as the plastic bucket.

Bottling Buckets - While you're looking into plastic buckets, you might consider purchasing a dedicated bottling bucket with a spigot attachment. These buckets are the same size and cost as a fermentation bucket, but they do not require a lid.

With one of these buckets, you can siphon off your fermented beer to separate it from yeast residue, dry-hop pouches, and any other items you don't want in the bottle. You can then pitch in the priming sugar all at once (recommended) before filling your bottles via the spigot tap.

Most homebrew starter kits already come with two buckets—one for fermentation and the other for priming and/or bottling—but neither is a dedicated bottling bucket and does not have a spigot tap. You are still perfectly able to siphon the beer into your bottles after priming without a spigot. I personally find the spigot more of a time-saver than a necessity.

Other Equipment

Much of the beer-making process revolves around the vessel you brew wort in and the container your wort ferments. Still, several tertiary items are crucial to ensure a successful batch. This section will discuss the additional equipment you will need and how much you should expect to pay for it.

Brew Bags – Even extract-based recipes might involve some milled grain, and beer brewing involves at least one hop infusion. You will undoubtedly need a few mesh brewing bags for these additions. Most kits will send you some disposable muslin bags. Still, I recommend you stock up on a personal cache, just if you want to get creative and experiment with extra hopping or other adjuncts.

A disposable mesh brew bag will cost you about a dollar. If you want to be a little greener and save some cash in the long run, you can invest in one or more $5 (£3) reusable steeping bags. These fine-mesh nylon brew bags have drawstrings that allow you to discard spent ingredients. You can then wash, sterilise, and dry the fabric, so it's ready for the next brew session.

Airlocks - As noted earlier, fermentation requires that carbon dioxide can escape the vessel as the sugar is converted. It also requires that oxygen and various other harmful agents be kept out. A small but essential tool for this is an airlock. They are designed to fit snugly into the hole in your bucket lid, bung, or carboy cap, to release gas while protecting the opening in your fermenter.

There are two types of airlocks:

- **S-Shape (or Bubble) Airlocks** is essentially a piece of thin tubing curved into an S with a water-chamber buffer. It's made in one piece and can be challenging to clean.
- **Three-Piece Airlocks** - this lock is composed of a cylindrical main chamber that you fill partly with water. You then place a floating bubbler on the water and cover the whole thing with a cap. The lock feeds carbon dioxide into the chamber, sending the bubbler bouncing. When that bubbler moves, you know the yeast is doing its work. This type of airlock is just marginally more expensive than the former.

The three-piece airlock is the best option here if only for it's easy to clean. Regardless, both airlocks are similarly inexpensive, and you can find a pack of three online for around \$5-\$7 (£4).

Alternatively, you may want to try some DIY alternatives, which often work equally as well. If you're using a carboy, you can attach a balloon, sandwich wrap, or even a condom over the opening, secured with rubber bands. Then, just poke some small holes for air to escape. Be careful, though—you don't want to be poking holes in all your condoms, or your brewing days may be over within as little as nine and a half months.

Siphons - Getting fermented wort from one place to another (known as racking) requires a siphon. By far, the best product for racking is a hand-pumped auto-siphon. Light and easy to sterilise, this is essentially a racking cane with an outer tube. Give it a couple of quick pumps. Your wort will flow evenly and continuously from the fermenter into the bottling bucket. No unnecessary exposure to impurities and no oxidation from splashing.

Super efficient auto-siphons cost as little as \$10 (£7).

The alternative to an auto-siphon, which I do not recommend, is using a racking cane and hose. The only options for starting the wort flow are to either fill the hose with water or suck on the end. Both options run a real risk of compromising your beer.

With all this pumping and sucking over with, we can get back to some more serious matters.

Thermometers and Hydrometers - Making beer can be somewhat scientific. Crafting a successful recipe doesn't just require good ingredients in proper ratios: it also involves time and careful calibration. Water needs to be maintained at specific temperatures for adding grains or malt extract. If you pitch your yeast into a wort that is too hot, you will certainly kill it. The balance of water and sugars in your wort also needs to be correct for yeast to ferment. This balance makes up the density of your liquid wort, which is better known as 'gravity' in brewing terms— a confusing idea for an astronaut.

When looking for a good brewing thermometer, you will want a product that can withstand high temperatures, be quickly read, and be easy to clean. Here are some options you could consider:

A standard glass thermometer will do the job. You can rest it in your brew pot and monitor the water temperatures. These usually retail in the $8-$12 (£6) range. Just be sure it's strong glass that can handle the heat you're working with. Shattered glass and mercury aren't great for drinking.

A Bi-Metal Dial Thermometer is equally effective. You can clip it on the edge of your pot and dip the probe into the liquid. The advantage here is you don't have to hold them near-boiling water, nor do you have to wait for them to get up to temperature. For the trouble they save over glass thermometers, they are a tad more expensive, costing around $12-$20 (£8).

Infrared Digital Thermometers were ubiquitous in the pandemic era as a quick, contactless way to check for fever. No more putting objects in various orifices like the good old days. To no surprise, they're also great for checking wort temperatures. They retail for around $20-$30 (£15) and are incredibly simple. You simply point and click, and a highly accurate number comes back almost instantly. Also, nothing comes into contact with your wort. Just be sure you're checking the liquid's temperature and not that of the container.

When making beer, you also have to measure your wort's gravity immediately after it goes in the fermenter, then re-check over the following days. A hydrometer is a long glass tube with a weighted ballast on one end. There is only one type, and a quality one will cost about $10-$15 (£7).

Readings on a hydrometer will also indicate when fermentation has ended and will give you a sense of your beer's alcohol-by-volume (ABV). The ABV of beer is dependent on factors such as fermentation temperature, gravity, and the quantity of yeast pitched, which will be discussed further in the next book, *Beer Brewing Bliss: All-Grain Brewing Mastery*.

Bottling Supplies

It's essential to ensure that you have all the necessary bottling supplies to get your brew over the finish line. To do this, you will first need bottles.

There are many types available to buy, and they are relatively inexpensive. The best types are as follows:

- **12 oz. Long Neck Glass Bottles** are a classic beer container. You will need to cap these using a bottle-capper. You can buy a 24-pack of these bottles online for around $20 (£15). It is best to use brown or green bottles to minimise light infiltration during conditioning.
- **Glass Swing Top Bottles** are generally 16 oz. in size. They require no capping, and their rubber-lined swing tops create a good seal. Prices vary, but ten swing tops will typically cost you $20 (£15). Although more expensive, they have the added benefit of being fully reusable.
- **Polyethylene Terephthalate (PET) Bottles** are plastic with a screw top, so they do not require capping. They will protect your brew against off-flavours but will not be as tightly sealed as a clinched cap. They retail for around a dollar each and are the most cost-effective bottle type. They are also suitable for comparing carbonation levels against a standard soda pop bottle from the local supermarket.

If you go with PET or Swing Top Bottles, you will not need to worry about buying caps and bottle capping tools. You will need to stock up on some bottle caps for long-neck glass bottles. Luckily, they are very affordable, around $5-$7 (£3) for a bag containing 150 caps.

As for capping tools, these fall into two categories:

- **Hand Cappers** look like robotic butterflies. They require a fair amount of elbow grease but will succeed in pinching the cap on tightly. One bottle is easy; twelve is a chore. By the time you reach your fortieth cap, you'll be ready for a nap. Most hand cappers retail for around $15-$20 (£10).
- **Bench Cappers** are the higher-end, higher-cost option. They vary in price from $40 to $100 (£30-£70). These are stationary models used by placing the bottle at the base and lowering the capping mechanism with a lever. The high price point buys you the ease of use. A one-handed slot machine motion is more

accessible than the workout you get from a hand capper.

A filling wand is a minor but handy tool that you'll need when bottling. This $8-$12 (£5) tube attaches to the spigot on your bottling bucket. It has a spring-loaded stopper at the end, so you can fill the wand with fermented wort and then depress the pin inside your bottle. This process ensures that you fill the bottle from the bottom, allowing minimal oxidation. It also limits flow into the bottle, so you don't overfill. A too-full bottle of priming wort is essentially a 'beer grenade', and we're not starting a war, right?!

To conclude, it may seem like a lot of effort purchasing all of these items for your first batch of beer, but remember that every piece of equipment will work for multiple batches. Some will even last you a lifetime of brewing—even if they were cheap, as some of my first items were. With this in mind, I encourage you to start optimising your homebrewing setup from the moment you make your first extract brew, mainly if you think it's a hobby that you will continue with long-term.

Chapter Three

Cleaning, Sanitising, and Sterilising

Long before beer was invented, ancient peoples would steep grains, sugars, and flowering plants in water and leave them to ferment. These early alcoholic drinks served as a way to make their liquid clean and potable. The grain-based drinks of old relied on microflora in the air to facilitate sugar conversion into ethanol. After all, nobody knew what yeast was until the 1800s, when Louis

Pasteur demonstrated their action on sugars. For many years, folks considered this process a gift from the heavens. Soaking the dough mixture in water and merely stowing it away in clay vessels for weeks was not the most sanitary process. The resulting brew would usually taste a little earthy and sour. However, there was some control over this process, and ancient brewers would have known precisely how long fermentation would take, even if they knew little of the reasons why.

Contrary to what you might think, such a seemingly dirty process is not always terrible. Many modern ale traditions involve spontaneous fermentation in open-air 'cool ship' fermentation vessels. Check out the fermenting room in Brussels at the 'Belgian Lambic Cantillon Brewery'. You'll see a somewhat dusty and stuffy environment. Here, the wort is ingesting a giant petri-dish of natural cultures from the air and using them to concoct the most exciting drinks. Some consider Cantillon's 'wild' ales delicious, although most would call them an acquired taste.

"So, why the history lesson?" you might ask.

This heedless process is great if you're an ancient Sumerian or a Brussels lambic maker. Still, suppose you're reading this book. In that case, you're probably gearing up to try your hand at your first malt extract recipe—and you probably aren't looking for it to come out smelling and tasting like apple cider vinegar. Obviously, you will want it to be as clean and crisp as the beer served to you in your finest local establishment. The key to this is proper cleaning and sanitation.

Beer Infection and the Flame-Out Rule

Before we get into the rudiments of sanitising your brewing equipment, let's look at a few potential risks of using non-sanitised equipment and discuss how to think logically about cleaning.

It's easy for the homebrewer to turn into Cinderella when thinking about cleaning and sterilising. You might find yourself inspecting every square inch of equipment for potentially deadly germs. The impulse towards perfect cleanliness is good, but it can be taken to extremes.

Let's explore the dangers of infected beer (or the lack thereof). Unless you accidentally dump a bottle of rat poison (or some other toxic agent) into your batch, an 'off' beer will not be dangerous. Standard microbial infiltration in your wort will, at worst, lead to a foul-tasting brew (although Belgian wild ale lovers may disagree). As mentioned earlier, many professional brewers have faced infection issues with various beer releases. Although not toxic, it is still a real shame that probably affected their bottom lines and PR strategies more than anything else.

Following the 'Flame-Out Rule' will make your sanitising strategy more straightforward. As I will discuss throughout the coming chapters, every brew has a point where you need to boil your wort, coinciding with the immersion of hops and any other adjuncts.

As a result, you can think of your beer making process as existing in 2 parts: pre-boil (before) and post-boil (after).

All equipment used before the boil should be clean but doesn't necessarily need to be surgically sterile.

As you probably already know, boiling kills most unwanted organisms that could potentially harm your beer (or your stomach, for that matter). You can even use clean utensils and containers from the kitchen that have not been relegated exclusively to beer-making. It is also helpful to note that you won't need much equipment before the wort boil in extract brewing. However, this will change dramatically as you advance to all-grain brewing.

In contrast, once the flame goes out on the boil, all equipment touching your wort from this point needs to be sanitised with extreme care. Your end goal should be to keep your gear as close to bacteria-free as possible. You will need to invest a little time and energy into cleaning and sanitising your post-boil equipment correctly.

Cleaning Your Equipment

Even the most intense cleaning regimes actually begin the same as any other. Start by giving each of your beer-making items the same attention you would give to a dish in your sink (or maybe a little more if you're a student). Be sure to scrub away any visible grime, sediment, or stains.

Using standard washing-up liquid is fine at this stage. It's only later when you're considering what you will use post-boil that you need to be a little more thorough than you would be after a family dinner.

Chemical Sanitation

Following cleaning, one of the best ways to ensure proper sanitary conditions for your brew is to select an excellent chemical sanitiser. These products come in both liquid and granulated forms but are used similarly. Ideally, you should aim for a no-rinse sanitiser so you can give your equipment a good soaking and then leave it out to air dry. Suppose you need to rinse with tap water after sanitising. In that case, you will likely undo much of your hard work, as even clean water still contains some bacteria.

Let's explore some of the most effective sanitising options.

Household Bleach - You probably already have this sitting around the house. Because bleach is abrasive with a distinct, penetrating scent, you must ensure that you dilute it sufficiently. Never put raw bleach onto brewing equipment, as it can cause damage! A good ratio is 2 ml of bleach to every 1 litre of water.

Unlike proprietary brewing sanitisers, bleach isn't great for metal. Prolonged exposure will cause your copper and steel instruments to become discoloured or even rust. You can soak your metals in a bleach solution for a short time, but then you must rinse them thoroughly to prevent damage. Only glass can be safely washed in a bleach solution for prolonged periods.

The pros and cons of using bleach in brewing are as follows:

- Bleach is relatively inexpensive, can be purchased locally, and is helpful outside of brewing. It is also an extremely powerful sanitiser. In contrast, the odour is penetrating, requires extensive rinsing, and can cause skin irritation if not used correctly. It will also tarnish metal items.
- Price range: A large bottle of bleach will run you about $3-$6 (£3).

OxiClean and Other Percarbonate Cleansers - Oxiclean is probably the best-known percarbonate cleaner. Others include B-Brite and One Step. These products use hydrogen peroxide to clean away dirt and grime from surfaces. While manufacturers market them as basic household cleansers, homebrewers have had great success using them to sanitise their tools.

A little goes a long way with percarbonate cleaners. Half a teaspoon of the powder will sanitise the inside of a water-filled 6.5-gallon carboy. Other pros and cons of using OxiClean are as follows:

- Percarbonate cleaners are potent and effective and leave very little residual smell. They are also biodegradable. In contrast, they require extensive rinsing and instances of skin irritation can occur.
- Price range: OxiClean retails for $9 (£6) for 3.5 lbs.

StarSan/ChemSan - These are the most popular liquid brewing sanitisers. They are no-rinse, odourless, and have no taste. A little also goes a long way with these liquids. You can effectively sanitise all your equipment with a ratio of 1.5 ml per one litre of water.

With StarSan and ChemSan, you can mix the sanitising solution, soak your freshly-cleaned items, empty them, and then leave them out to air dry. Other pros and cons of using StarSan/ChemSan are as follows:

- StarSan and ChemSan require no rinsing as these cleaners are scentless and devoid of taste. These chemicals are optimised for beer-making. In contrast, they are more expensive than other sanitisers and can foam up when mixed.
- Price range: 16 ounces of StarSan or ChemSan costs around $12 (£9).

PBW and VWP Sanitisers - PBW and VWP are both granulated powder sanitisers. Like StarSan and ChemSan, they have zero residual taste. The product dissolves quickly in warm water and uses a similar mixing ratio to StarSan or ChemSan.

Unlike any other option in this chapter, a well-blended PBW solution resembles water because a good amount of it can be ingested relatively consequence-free. While I wouldn't recommend drinking it from the glass, I have no problems leaving some residue in my three-piece airlock or racking fermented wort through a hose that still has droplets of PBW inside. Other pros and cons of PBW and VWP are as follows:

- With PBW or VWP, rinsing is recommended, although both are devoid of scent and taste. They are also biodegradable and come in both powder and tablet form. The only drawback is they can leave a (non-toxic) residue behind.
- Price range: One pound of PMW powder costs about $10 (£7).

Iodophor - Iodine-based solutions like Iodophor are incredibly fast-acting and effective. Like some other chemical sanitisers, Iodophor requires no rinsing after application. It has the added bonus of working just as effectively with cold water as with hot.

The recommended ratio for Iodophor is approximately 0.75 mL to one litre of water.

Unlike the other sanitisers on this list, it does not make a clear solution. Anyone who's ever been stitched up after an injury knows the russet brown colour of iodine solution. You will get that same tone in an Iodophor mixture, and it is likely to stain light fabrics and plastic upon exposure. Other pros and cons of Iodophor are as follows:

- Iodophor works incredibly fast. Most sanitising takes only a couple of minutes, and not much product is needed to achieve proper sanitation. Iodophor also works with cold water. In contrast, this sanitiser will stain plastic, making your fermenting and bottling buckets harder to clean later. It can also impart a metallic off-flavour.
- Price range: Four ounces of Iodophor sells for $4-$8 (£6).

These items will get the job done, although my personal favourite is PBW powder. It stores well in a compact container and produces a clear, no-taste, no-smell, and no-foam solution. The residue is also non-toxic in moderate amounts.

Use cooled boiled water to minimise the risk of re-introducing bacteria to your freshly sanitised items during rinsing. Any substantive bacteria will have been killed during boiling. You won't need to worry about undermining your own hard labour.

Heat Sterilisation

There is another way to thoroughly sanitise the equipment that does not involve any sanitising solutions for those who don't fancy having your beer with a side of sanitising chemicals. As already discussed, boiling can kill microorganisms living in the water. The same is true for items placed under high temperatures, like an oven or kiln. Both wet and dry heat can sometimes prove even more effective than chemical options. This is because steam and hot air can penetrate areas that liquid cannot—for example, cracks in plastic or wood where bacteria can multiply.

After cleaning the visible gunk from your equipment, you have the following heat sterilisation options:

Steam Heating - Recent pandemic life has made people more conscientious about their health. With time on their hands, some will have rushed to the store to buy a new pressure cooker to cook the healthy (and delicious) meals they'd always dreamt of. If you're one of those who didn't own an 'Instant Pot' before, there's a good chance you've got one now. Even if it was a poor substitute for your favourite takeaway, at least you would have managed a good curry with minimal effort. And even if you never use it for cooking ever again, it could still come in handy for your home brewing endeavours.

Pressure cookers and autoclaves are excellent ways to sterilise brewing equipment. Steam serves the same purpose that boiling does when it comes to killing bacteria because, well, steam is just boiling water in gas form. If you were to run your steam cooker at 257°F (125°C), you could thoroughly sanitise an item in twenty minutes.

You could consider using the dishwasher for larger containers and bottles that may not do well under pressure (or won't fit in your 'Instant Pot'). Running a lengthy high-temperature cycle without detergent will achieve similar results. I do appreciate that finding an empty dishwasher when you have a family of four may bring some substantial logistical challenges.

Dry Heating - Your oven will not be as efficient as an autoclave, but it can do the job well if you give it a little extra time. If you place your equipment in an oven at 338°F (170°C), it will be thoroughly sterilised in an hour. If you have more time to spare, run your range overnight at 248°F (120°C). This will be much gentler on your equipment, unlike your partner after a few good homebrews.

Cover the openings with a piece of aluminium foil to prevent internal contamination of bottles after heating, and leave them covered until you're ready to fill and cap.

Just for those who didn't make the grade in secondary school physics, you need to exercise some common sense when heat-treating your equipment. For example, some plastics will only withstand a specific temperature, so an autoclave or an oven may not be the best place. You don't want your nice new auto-siphon to end up like the toy army man you liquefied under a magnifying glass as a child. Similarly, you don't want to expose your glassware to large fluctuations in temperature, as they will likely crack and/or shatter during cooling. This could ruin brew day, sending you to the hospital with third-degree burns and glass in your hand.

An easy way to avoid personal injury whilst handling very hot objects is to have a pair of insulated gloves to hand (no pun intended). You will also need clean towels and plenty of ventilation.

The Bottom Line

It doesn't matter how flawlessly you execute your brew: your beer could be ruined if you use unclean equipment. Maintaining a sterile brewing inventory means thinking carefully about which tools need to only be cleaned (pre-boil) and which require thorough sanitation (post-boil). As discussed, there are many tools and products that make sterilising your equipment incredibly easy. These tried and tested methods will give you peace of mind and make you confident that your beer will come out just as intended.

Moreover, it will do you well to be fastidious in your cleaning. Suppose you're the kind of person that likes to grow weird and wonderful moulds on two-week-old plates or leave dishes soaking until it's time to wash them properly. In that case, you'll probably need to become your own nagging roommate.

Every second that malt residue, yeast trub, or hop remnants hang around on your fermenter or brewing spoon is another opportunity for bacteria to propagate. Even the best sanitising solution will have difficulty getting the surface sterile if you leave them there too long. With this in mind, here are some simple do's and don'ts regarding cleaning and sanitising on brew day:

Cleaning & Sanitising Do's

- Clean up immediately after you're done with the brewing equipment. Don't give the bacteria time to collect, settle, and propagate.
- Use household sponges, dish-washing bleach, and anti-bacterial detergent to clean up after each stage.

- Use a dishwasher, if available, for any items that you use during and before your boil.
- Invest in the necessary cleaning implements for your brewing and fermenting equipment. This includes brushes for your bottle, carboy, and tubing. It could also mean bottle trees for drying or the drill attachment for advanced demijohn scrubbing. It's a lot more economical to get the correct cleaning supplies than to replace bacteria-ridden equipment.
- Keep scrubbing and rinsing until the equipment looks spotless. If you can see gunk and grime, the item is not clean.
- Have a clean drying area ready. You don't want your newly cleaned equipment sitting in the prior evening's chicken grease.
- Give your equipment an additional cleaning before your next batch. The time between brews allows many opportunities for beer-spoiling microbes to collect from the environment.
- Keep a container of sanitising solution nearby to rest stirrers, thermometers, and any other equipment.
- Follow the directions on your cleaning products strictly. Residual soap and bleach on a

pot, spoon, or brush can be as detrimental as a residual mess.

Cleaning & Sanitising Don'ts

- Avoid scouring brushes and pads, especially on plastic items. They create minor abrasions on your equipment where bacteria can collect and multiply.
- Don't use cheap and overly perfumed washing-up liquid. It will be ineffective at killing bacteria and may cause off-flavours in your batch.
- Never dry your equipment with a dishrag. Doing so will effectively spread more bacteria onto items you've just sanitised. You're spreading this horrid army of microbes across everything you wipe. Anything you sanitise by hand should be air-dried, either in a dedicated rack for brewer's glassware or on a clean patch of the counter with fresh-from-the-package paper towels.

- Don't use beer-making equipment for food or other household purposes unless it's only part of the pre-boil brewing process.

Now that we have the tools and knowledge to ensure a sanitary process, let's get down to the fun stuff. You're ready to brew your first malt extract beer!

Chapter Four

Making the Wort

The big moment has arrived. You have your beer ingredients, your equipment is clean and ready to go, and you have cleared an afternoon to brew. So let's get started!

The first step on the road to a homemade beer is turning water into the wort. The wort is the unfermented elixir loaded up with glucose, fructose, sucrose, maltose, and maltotriose. However, making a good wort is about creating sugars for the yeast to ferment. The kinds of malt, hops, and adjunct ingredients you add to your brew will ultimately contribute to your final beer's appearance, aroma, mouthfeel, and taste.

So, let's dig into how wort is made without further delay.

From Water to Wort

Generally, the wort is created by steeping malted barley grains in water. Whether you go down the extract malt route or the all-grain route, you will eventually arrive at the same point with a delicious wort pot ready for fermentation.

Mashing, Lautering, and Sparging - As an all-grain brewer, the process is more involved than it would be as an extract brewer. You would submerge your milled and malted barley grains in hot water, then take them through a lautering process, which is the separation of liquid from the grain. Firstly, you would drip water continuously through the grain bed to remove any excess fermentable sugars from the spent grains in your mash tun. Continuous water cycling (better known as sparging) through malted barley leeches most of the flavour, colour, body, and fermentable materials needed for a good wort. This entire process is known in the industry as 'mashing'.

All-Grain Wort Vs. Extract Wort - At this stage, you will be working from a malt extract recipe, so understanding the all-grain mash process is purely academic. You will not need a dedicated mash tun with a lauter plate to steep and separate liquor from grain, as this has been done for you.

Of course, this makes your wort-creation process markedly simpler. Essentially, you will be heating brewing water to a suitable temperature and pitching in a 'pre-mashed' malt extract. If your recipe calls for some milled speciality grain infusions, you won't need to lauter or sparge. Like hops, these infusions can be added via a steeping bag.

Here is the equipment you will need to make your malt extract wort:

- A large cooking pot or dedicated brew pot, or kettle

- A sizeable stirring spoon, ideally slotted, meshed, or perforated
- A cooking thermometer, if one is not already built into your brewing kettle
- Steeping bags for speciality malts
- A clean water source
- Two bags of ice cubes (for wort cooling), unless you have a cooling coil already

As mentioned in Chapter 3, you want all of this equipment to be clean before the brew. However, it does not need to be thoroughly sanitised or heat-sterilised at this stage. The only possible exception to this rule would be the lid to your brewing vessel, which will come into contact with the cooled wort right before you transfer it to your primary fermenter. I would highly recommend sterilising the lid before putting it on the cooling vessel.

Overview of Ingredients

Most, if not all, of your malt, will come as a molasses-like liquid (wet malt) or a dry powder similar to confectioners sugar (dry malt, or

DME). Malt extract purchased from a reputable producer will impart the same tastes, aromas, and colouration as milled grain. Using extract will probably lead to a more refined end product since it removes a lot of the fine-tuning and guesswork involved in the mashing process.

You can expect your extract recipe to come with malt syrup and/or dry powder in a bag or bottle. Your recipe might also include a package (or several) of milled malted speciality grains. You will also be given hops, which will most likely come in the form of compressed pellets instead of whole cones. Contemporary East Coast-style IPAs may also make use of hop oil or powders. Each recipe will come with hops dedicated to giving the correct level of bitterness to whatever beer you're making.

Depending on the style, other adjuncts may be added during your wort creation. Good examples of such ingredients are milk, sugar, or maltose. These additions can bolster a silky, full-bodied mouthfeel without increasing the alcohol content of the beer.

Strike Water

Sounds dangerous, but strike water is simply the name given to any water used in the brewing process. When we talk about making beer, our thoughts naturally gravitate towards ingredients like chocolaty dark malts, citric hops, or spicy yeast strains. Still, the most populous ingredient in beer is often overlooked. In fact, over 90% of the beer you make is water, so we must give it some careful consideration.

Hill Farmstead Brewing in Greensboro Bend, Vermont, has been named the best brewery in the world by multiple independent beer journals. It uses water from a well located on the founding family's century-old farmland. This water is well known for making deliciously bright IPAs and funky Saisons.

Similarly, the brewers at St. Bernardus Brewery in Belgium make world-class abbey ales using water pumped from 150 metres below ground. This groundwater originated from rainfall during the time of Joan of Arc, giving it a mineral profile perfect for this type of ale.

You may be thinking, "This is all well and good, but I don't have access to 600-year-old water". Don't worry; you don't actually need it to make a decent beer. Here are some factors you might want to consider before filling up your brew pot with strike water.

Purity - First and foremost, your water should look, smell, and taste pure. Suppose you're fortunate enough to live in an area with excellent tap-water quality. In that case, you might not need to do anything other than turn on the faucet. If not, many impurities can be sifted out using water filters, and even more will burn off during the boil. However, if your water smells off, whether, from organic material or chlorine, it will likely cause 'off' smells and flavours in your wort. In this case, you are better off buying a few gallons of bottled water from your local store.

Ions, Alkalinity, and Hardness - In general, the best strike water is:

- Moderately hard, meaning it contains some calcium and magnesium.

- Of a pH that will work well with the malt bill of your recipe.

To clarify what this means for you, let's review some simple chemistry.

At an atomic level, you can think of strike water containing a series of ions or atom groups with positive or negative charges. Without getting into every type of ion and its effect on wort, let's simply say that these ions in water function like the treble/bass balance knobs on your home sound system. Suppose the other beer ingredients are the music. In that case, weighting your water with specific ions will accentuate one component or another. For example, water with a high ratio of sulphate ions will emphasise hop content. In contrast, water with high chloride content will boost malty sweetness.

Good strike water should only be moderately hard, and adding softening tablets to hard tap water may compound your problems, leaving you with water that is too alkaline. For example, the ideal pH range for malt enzymes to convert starch into fermentable sugars during an all-grain mash is around 5, which is slightly acidic. As the addition of malted grains also tends to raise the pH of water, this will likely do enough to get you in the suitable range for good starch conversion. Although not much of a problem for the extract brewer, it is helpful to bear in mind for later.

Optimising your Strike Water - It's best not to drive yourself crazy over ions, alkalinity, and hardness when working with a malt recipe. Your adage should be "do no harm" rather than striving for absolute perfection. The extract producer has already conducted the mash under the correct water conditions and extracted the necessary things from the grain.

This means much less work, although I would recommend buying an inexpensive pH test kit (for as little as $5/£4) and a water hardness test kit (around $8-10/£7). You want to aim for a pH of 5.2-5.6 and a total hardness of 150 ppm or higher for your strike water. Suppose your water's pH is significantly higher than the desired range. In this case, you may consider purchasing a brewing pH stabiliser, which retails for $15-$20 (£12) per pound.

You can also add mineral products like brewing salts to the water to increase its hardness or to boost ions for bitterness or maltiness.

Anyone who owns a hot tub will find this balancing act a 'piece of cake' in comparison—and, by the way, if you don't own a hot tub already, I would highly recommend getting one. What better place to sit and drink a freshly made homebrew with friends on a winter's day?!

In contrast, if you are a beginner brewer and think that all this may be too much fiddling about or will cause you additional stress, you can usually skip this part entirely. As long as your water is clean, neutral-tasting, and not overly alkaline, you can confidently proceed with making your wort. You'll have plenty of opportunities to experiment with the chemistry of your strike water as you get into more complex all-grain brewing.

Selecting and Adding Malts

Before discussing the different types of malt you can use, it would perhaps be sensible to talk a little about how barley is malted, including steeping, germination, and kilning. But because it's not so relevant at this stage in your brewing career, I will save that one for 'All-grain Brewing Mastery'.

In this book, I will divulge two main classes of malt used in beer making: base and speciality malts.

Base Malts – Base malt essentially makes up the 'lion's share of the malt you add to your strike water. In an extract recipe, your base malt will be entirely made up of syrup or powder. Base malt contributes to your beer's primary hue, smell, and taste. Still, its most significant contribution to the recipe is its fermentable material. Different types of base malt are derived from different strains of barley, often originating from various regions of the world. Because these bases impart different colours and flavours, the malt you use will be determined by the style of beer you want to make.

All base malts come from two-row and six-row barley (simply referring to the number of kernels present on the head of the barley plant). Due to such differences in plant morphology, not all base malts will look the same or add the same qualities to a beer.

Here is a simple table to sum up the common types of base malt and their uses:

- **Pilsner Malt** - This two-row barley base is lightly kilned to a golden finish. The malt's character is bright and delicate. Used not only in lighter lagers but also in blonde and pale ales.
- **Pale Ale Malt** - Also two-row in origin, this malt is darker than Pilsner. The toasted cereal character makes it a perfect backbone for any hoppy pale ale.
- **Vienna Malt** - This is a fully toasted six-row barley malt. It produces a full-bodied, robust sweetness. Used in Bocks.
- **Munich Malt** - Amber-coloured and two-row derived, Munich malt provides a rich, toffee-like base. Common in Oktoberfests and other dark German beers.
- **Wheat Malt** - Perhaps not surprisingly from the name, this is not barley. Wheat malt is very popular, providing a robust, estery protein base in Wheat Ales and Hefeweizens.

Speciality Malts – If base malts provide the soul of a beer, speciality malts are the flourishes. They can be explicitly used to add unique flavours and aromas to a beer. Along with hop additions, this is where brewers can really get creative.

In an extract brew recipe, speciality grains need to be steeped (soaked) in your strike water at 158°F (70°C) for approximately 15-30 minutes. This will usually be the first thing you do on brew day before boiling and adding your malt—unless your recipe states otherwise. Steeping temperatures and times will also differ from recipe to recipe as they're dependent on the type of grain you're using. Once complete, you will be able to fish out bags of spent grain using your brewing spoon/paddle before boiling. A good thermometer will also come in handy at this stage.

It is probably comforting to note that steeping a speciality malt is similar to performing a 'partial mash', which will be discussed in the next book. You will use more grain than you would whilst steeping small quantities of speciality malt; however, this is a positive step towards all-grain brewing practices.

Speciality malts can be divided into two groups: caramel (sometimes called crystal) and roasted.

Caramel malts undergo a heating process that caramelises their sugars. Roasted malts go through an additional heating process, leaving them looking darker and sporting coffee and dark chocolate notes.

Here is a rundown of some standard speciality malts that you may find included in your extract recipe:

- **Caramel 60 Malt** - This is probably the most prevalent caramel malt. This medium-kilned malt provides succulent-sweet notes that play well in various styles, from English Bitters to Stouts.
- **Caramel 120 Malt** - Caramel 120 is darker and more roasted than 60. Its toffee flavour is more burnt. Favoured in strong brews like Barley wines and Doppelbocks.
- **Special B Malt** - This caramel malt is nutty and redolent of stewed stone fruit. It's used in Stouts, Porters, and Barley wines.
- **Chocolate Malt** - A roasted malt that imparts dark chocolate flavour and a reddish tone. You won't be surprised to hear that Brown Ales, Porters, and Stouts all use it.

- **Black Patent Malt** - Another mainstay of the Stout, this roasted malt is as dark as grains get. Its espresso notes can edge over charcoal if you accidentally use too much.
- **Roasted Barley** - Technically, this isn't malt. It is heavily fired plain barley, commonly used in Stouts for the baker's chocolate character it imparts.

Once you've finished steeping speciality malts, it's time to turn up the heat.

Two essential things you want to avoid at this point are boil-overs and sticking. This means that, at some points, you may need to drop the heat under your water or even kill the flame entirely. You also want to stir as you pour in your extract. LME will sink straight to the bottom of the tun unless you stir continuously, and DME tends to clump. So make sure to keep your spoon/paddle moving, or you'll end up with a charred, gummy mess at the bottom of your brewing pot.

As your wort merrily bubbles away, you will want to get ready to add your hops.

Selecting and Adding Hops

Hops are the third ingredient added to wort after water and malts. These flowering plants will impart some very distinct flavours to your beer. Just as many types of malts can be combined to create a particular style profile, many different strains of hops can be combined to do the same.

Hops are also what separates beer from all other drinks. Plenty of beverages—most notably, whiskey—use malted grain in their production. However, hops are unique to beer and give the finished product its trademark bitterness, plus those resinous, piney, citric, and floral notes that all beer lovers crave. Moreover, the bitterness, flavour, or aroma delivered to the wort depends on the time that the hops are added and for how long. You also need to pay particular care to pitch in the correct amount of hops so that your wort leeches the right components.

Don't worry, though. Suppose you're working from a pre-packaged extract recipe; there will be specific instructions on when to add particular hops during your boil session.

Describing Hops – The hop is the flower of the - *Humulus lupulus* plant (a.k.a. the 'common hop'), which is part of the Cannabaceae family of hemp plants. When harvested, hop buds look like small, pliable green pine cones. Each hop flower has lupulin glands that contain and secrete particular resins and oils.

Now you may be thinking, "Sounds very similar to cannabis", and you'd be right. Due to a genetic linkage, both hops and cannabis contain many of the same resins and oils, most derived from chemicals called terpenes and terpenoids. These give hops and cannabis their characteristic smell and why, if you were blindfolded, the scent of a very hoppy ale could easily be mistaken for that of a freshly rolled joint.

However, these plants have one notable difference: hops lack the enzymes necessary to convert terpenes into THC (the psychoactive compound found in cannabis plants). A crying shame, and you may be asking, "Why don't we use cannabis in brewing"?

Obviously, there are certain legalities surrounding this, but thankfully, the Canadians are one step ahead. Since the Canadian legalisation of cannabis back in 2018, brewers there have experimented with using cannabis buds in place of classic hops. Although this experiment didn't produce desirable results (especially in terms of taste), I believe they have recently succeeded in making gluten- and alcohol-free cannabis-infused beer using a different recipe altogether. Maybe inspiration for another book when the time is right.

Going further back in history, the Roman naturalist Pliny the Elder made the first known reference to hops in his Naturalis Historia in 77 AD, shortly before he was reduced to ash in the volcanic disaster at Pompeii. For his achievement, one of the most beloved beers on Earth is named after him: Russian River's Pliny the Elder IPA. Of course, no expense is spared on the hops for this recipe.

However, it wasn't until the eighth century that brewers began using hops in their fermented drinks. In the 15th and 16th centuries, the international hop trade became a political flashpoint. The English banned its use in commercial brewing, and the Germans squabbled over its taxation. However, by the 17th century, most bureaucratic and diplomatic issues were resolved, and hops had found a permanent home in the brewery.

Effect of Hops on Wort – Hops add bitterness and unique "green" flavours to a beer.

The glands in each hop flower contain the following:

- Alpha acids impart bitterness to the wort
- Beta acids affect the aroma of wort
- Essential oils give the wort a characteristic smell
- Flavonoids affect the taste

Typically, the first hops you pitch into the boiling wort will be for bittering. These hops contain more alpha acids (AA). They remain in the wort throughout the entire boil, generally between one and one-and-a-half hours.

Subsequent hop immersions are usually pitched in with fifteen to thirty minutes left until flameout and impart only slight bitterness but lots of additional flavours.

There is also a common practice in brewing known as 'dry-hopping', which involves additional hop infusions added during fermentation. This practice has been especially prevalent recently in producing more hoppy IPAs.

Bitterness in Beer – Bitterness is measured on a scale of International Bittering Units, or IBUs. For over a century, the IBU scale has advised folk on how bitter a brew is to taste. The scale begins at 0 and has no ceiling, though most beers fall in the 0-120 IBU range. Sour beers, wheat, and light American lagers are at the lower end of the scale. At the top, you will find the notoriously intense American barley wines and most IPAs.

It's worth noting that a sea change has occurred recently on the upper end of the IBU scale. In the 1990s and 2000s, many craft brewers were involved in what I can only describe as an IBU' arms race'. The West coast pale ale model pioneered by brewers like Sierra Nevada, Stone Brewing, and Ballast Point led to IPAs being produced with face-scrunching bitterness ratings of over 120.

However, in the last decade, an alternative East coast model has reached ascendancy, led by New England brewers like the Alchemist, Hill Farmstead, Lawson's Finest Liquids, and Tree House Brewing. These ales forgo all but the most basic bitterness hopping, favouring multiple late boil and dry-hop infusions. The resulting beers have much lower IBU counts but explosive amounts of candied citrus and pine needle flavours.

Hop Products and Varieties – Hop pellets are made by hammer pressing dried hop cones into a fine powder and then compressing. Today, most professional brewers use hop pellets, as they are easier to package and have a longer shelf life. Pellets are more efficient than cones since the material in their glands is already exposed to the air— giving a larger surface area for the wort to work on.

Brewing efficiency is one of the decisive advantages of using hop pellets. Everything you put into your strike water will soak some of it up, leading to an overall loss of water over the entire brewing process. Whole-cone hops suck up more liquid than their compressed counterparts, meaning less wort is left at the end of your boil. On the other hand, some brewers argue that the fresh whole-cone hops work best because their leaves act as natural controlled-release filters.

In recent years, there have been groundbreaking scientific advances in hop production. Notably, Yakima Chief Hops (YCH) in Washington, between 2014 and 2016, developed a novel cryogenic hop-processing technology. This process allowed the extraction of lupulin, the yellow powder-like substance produced by the hop plant. Lublin contains much of the terpene-based resins and aromatic oils that add flavour to your beer. Since then, YCH has used this unique process to produce a new hop pellet containing more concentrated amounts of lupulin, meaning you can use less, save on time, and have less waste material hanging around in your brewing vessels.

Other than previously mentioned, there are many more natural hop varieties available. To be precise, there are currently over 80 different strains grown and processed worldwide. While I couldn't possibly give a complete account of all 80, here is a rundown of some of the most popular and well-used hop varieties:

Bittering Hops –

- **Chinook -** A whopping 14% Alpha acid content with biting forest-type notes. Popular in Lagers and Pale Ales.
- **CTZ (Columbus, Tomahawk, and Zeus)** - Zesty and herbal. Adds a delicate floral note to dark beers like Stouts but can also be used in Pales.
- **Magnum -** Known for its raw bittering power and minimal aromatics. Used in traditional English-style ales.
- **Nugget -** A contemporary bittering hop with lots of grassy, weedy aromas. Good in Pale Ales, Ambers, and Stouts.

Flavouring hops –

- **Cascade/Centennial -** These two hops, developed and grown in the Pacific Northwest of the US, are quintessential West Coast aromatic hops. They are the lupulin stars of Sierra

Nevada's Pale Ale and Bell's Two Hearted Ale, respectively, full of tangerine and pine needle flavour.

- **Citra** - As intensely juicy as its name suggests, this hop is a mainstay of the East Coast hazy IPA.
- **Fuggle/Golding** - Herbal, woody, and flowery. These are the classic English Ale flavour hops. Every world-class Bitter uses one of these two varieties.
- **Mosaic/Simcoe** - Two hip American IPA hops, Mosaic and Simcoe, are common complements to Citra. They have plenty of orange and passion fruit to them and a lot of wood and cannabis flavour.
- **Saaz** - Germany's finest noble hop. It's a bit spicy and a bit earthy. You will recognise its delicate, crisp presence in Pilsner Urquell.

Again, these are just a few popular options to start thinking about the different hops available. Working with extract brew recipes is a great way to get used to the flavours and aromas produced by various hops before moving on to all-grain brewing.

Growing and Harvesting Hops at Home – Growing your own cones at home is an excellent option for those wanting to go off the beaten path with their hop bill. Hops grow in loam-rich soil with a pH between 6.0 and 7.5. They do incredibly well between the 35th and 55th parallels, which explains why there is such a rich hop growing industry in mainland Europe and the United States.

Suppose your climate and soil are amenable to hop growing; you can go to either a homebrew shop or nursery to purchase the rhizomes for your desired strain(s). These plants grow well in partial shade and require trussing to prop them up as they become taller. Once a hop plant is well established, it will live for around 25-50 years. A rather sad thought, maybe, for the ageing homebrewer.

Hop harvesting happens typically in August and September. You must check the cones carefully to ensure they're ready to be picked. Here are some tell-tale signs that a hop is ready for harvest:

- It springs back to its full shape quickly after being squeezed
- It smells pungent and grassy

- It makes a squeaking sound when rolled in your fingers close to your ear
- It's sticky at the tip
- It has a yellowish substance on the outside (the lupulin)

You will pick your hops by hand in your first year of growing. After that, your plant should be large enough for you to cut whole bines at once. Wear protective gloves and long sleeves since too much direct exposure to these cones can cause skin irritation.

Next, you will need to dry your hops for use in brewing. Because hops contain 80% water off the bine, that vast bucket of cones you've just harvested will decrease in size dramatically after drying. You can dry your hops in a food dehydrator or ventilated oven. You can also lay them on a screen in direct sunlight for two to three days, provided you are privileged enough to live in a place where you actually see some decent sunlight for more than three days a year. Obviously, I don't, hence the metaphorical 'bitterness' in my tone.

If you choose to use a ventilated oven or dehydrator, make sure the temperature doesn't exceed 60°C. Once the stem of the hop is brittle, and the cone leaves are papery, your hops are ready for brewing!

The best way to store dried hop cones is in a vacuum-sealed bag. You can also use zip-locking food bags with as much air squeezed out as possible. Hops should be packaged in 1 oz and 2 oz increments for easier deployment later. They can also be stored in your freezer for up to a year.

A Final Note on Malt and Hops

If you're a beer lover—which I imagine is why you are reading this book—you will know there are scores of disparate beer styles, from clean, crisp Bavarian lagers to thick, confectionery-like imperial stouts. Each kind of beer uses different types, combinations, and quantities of malt and hops.

For example, a high-ABV Quadruple Ale might use more malted barley than an ESB. Quadruples are heavy, boozy beers with lots of toffee and fig notes.

They require lots of fermentable sugar and many barley varieties.

By the same token, an American IPA will require more hop infusions than an English Porter because hops are the dominant flavour agent in IPAs.

Don't be surprised if two recipes have widely different malt and hop bills. As you move from packaged kits to your own recipes, you can start to experiment with varying levels of complementary ingredients. That's where things get really fun!

Chilling Your Wort

This is definitely no time to chill out. Once you have added your bittering and flavouring hops and reached the end of your brew, it is time to kill the flame.

First, you need to cool the wort to a temperature that won't kill your yeast. Ale yeast works best in wort sitting at 68-72° F (20–22° C). Lager yeast needs a wort closer to 45-57° F (7–14° C). You don't want your wort to be any more than 54° F (12° C) hotter than the yeast you pitch in.

Cooling quickly after flameout will reduce the likelihood of bacteria forming and prevent many off-flavours in the final beer. Remember, now that the boil is done, everything that comes into contact with your wort must be thoroughly sanitised.

Next are a few ways you can effectively cool your wort to the correct temperature:

Topping Off with Water - Many extract recipes require you to brew a concentrated wort, then top it off with water after flameout. You might find that your brew day involves a three-gallon wort boil topped off with two gallons of cold water. This top-off will do much of the wort cooling for you. You can even assist this process by refrigerating the water overnight. Be sure that both the water and its containers are adequately sanitised. Much like rinsing, it's better to use pre-boiled water for this process.

Sink Cooling - Most kitchen sinks can fit a 3-5 gallon brew pot. Cover your wort and place it in a bath of iced water. Sink cooling requires approximately 3-4 pounds of ice. You can speed up the cooling process by regularly stirring and cycling the cooling water. You should also stir your cooling wort with a sanitised spoon/paddle. Once the outer of the pot can be touched without burning your hand, check the wort temperature with a thermometer.

Wort-Chillers - The downside of sink chilling is that it takes time. If you want something that will work faster (advised), you can purchase a wort chiller. Chillers are essentially coiled copper tubes that you submerge into hot wort. You then attach a cold-water tap to one end and a drainage tube. When you turn on the tap, the continuous cold water flow cools the wort quickly from within. A significantly more efficient process than using an ice bath, albeit a little harsher on the wallet.

If you have a more advanced brew kettle, you can opt to use a counter-flow chiller. These coiled copper devices contain a tube within a tube. The inner tube carries wort while the outer has cold water. A counter-flow chiller connects to your brew kettle's fixture and deposits cooled wort directly into your fermenter.

Depending on size, wort chillers retail for anywhere from \$50-\$100 (£35-£70). Counter-flow chillers cost a little more at \$100-\$150 (£70-£100).

If you would like to use a wort chiller but don't have the money to invest in a purpose-built chiller, you can make one yourself using copper pipes and plastic tubing. In the next book, "All-Grain Brewing Mastery", there is a section detailing exactly how to do this.

Starting Warm - Some homebrewers choose not to thoroughly chill their wort before pitching in yeast. They cool their wort to within 3–6° C of their yeast temperature, then proceed straight to fermentation. The logic here is that warm wort will begin fermentation more quickly, reducing the likelihood of bacterial infection. However, this is a dud notion.

Like yeast, bacteria propagate more quickly in warm liquid than in cold. So your yeast is multiplying faster, yes, but so are stray bacteria that managed to infiltrate the vessel. Bacteria also move much faster than yeast, meaning there will eventually be more bacteria than yeast in your fermenter. More bacteria means more competition for your yeast cells and more 'off' flavours. For this reason, I recommend that you avoid 'starting warm'. You don't gain any substantial benefit, and you also risk scorching your yeast.

This brings us to the next stage of our beer making journey. It's time for your wort to become beer.

Chapter Five

Fermentation

The beer-making monks of central Europe realised that the sludge at the bottom of their bottles, known as trub, could be retained and transferred to the next batch of beer. This process sped up fermentation and achieved a certain level of flavour consistency from batch to batch. It was arguably 'just good luck that they realised this through hundreds of years of trial and error, and at least one person should be praised for their intuition. Of course, the monks knew that the sludge was important, but the science did not exist to explain why. Consequently, they decided that this was something of a divine nature, and thus, they called it '*godisgood*'.

This all changed in 1680 when Antonie van Leeuwenhoek, 'the father of microbiology', viewed yeast globules under a microscope for the first time. He was a Dutch scientist who was best known for his work in microscopy and was instrumental in bringing the field of microbiology to the forefront of modern science. Leeuwenhoek was also responsible for giving a general name to the microorganisms he observed. He called them 'animalcules' (tiny animals), although this is the English translation from the Dutch, '*dierkens*'. Although Leeuwenhoek didn't know much about fermentation, his work helped set a firm grounding for scientists like Louis Pasteur.

Louis Pasteur was a French microbiologist and the founder of the famous Pasteur Institute in Paris. You may have heard his name because of the 'pasteurisation' of milk, which was pioneered by Louis Pasteur himself. The institute was founded in 1887 and has since been the place of many ground-breaking scientific discoveries, including that of the 'Yersinia pestis' bacteria responsible for causing bubonic plague outbreaks in Europe hundreds of years earlier. In addition to his achievements mentioned above, Louis Pasteur was the first to demonstrate experimentally that yeast cells were responsible for the process of fermentation.

Fermentation is the name given to converting glucose to carbon dioxide gas and ethanol (ethyl-alcohol) under anaerobic conditions. This process is known as anaerobic respiration, which happens in the absence of oxygen. Like yeast and bacteria, some organisms can survive for long periods using only this type of respiration.

For the non-scientists, respiration is a process that happens in the cells of all living organisms. It is categorised by the conversion of sugars into energy: either in the presence or absence of oxygen. All living cells need this energy to survive. No respiration, no life.

The primary respiration type in both human and yeast cells is aerobic, meaning oxygen is present.

You may have heard of doing 'aerobics'. This is where the name comes from if you didn't already know. Human cells can also carry out anaerobic respiration for a short time but do so differently from microbes like yeast.

Being knowledgeable on fermentation, in 1856, Louis Pasteur was called to help a local distiller named Bigo, whose work involved fermenting beetroot sugars into alcohol. Bigo was having problems with one particular batch, which instead of producing alcohol, was creating something resembling sour milk. Pasteur found that Bigo's vessels of sour milk-like drink contained vast amounts of lactic acid. When he analysed the microbes in each vessel, he noticed that the lactic acid vessel had more bacteria than yeast. This discovery led Pasteur to realise that lactic acid production was the work of anaerobic bacteria and alcohol production was the work of yeast. For this reason, if you get a 'soured' batch of beer, the off taste is likely caused by lactic acid-producing bacteria.

Today, we understand that pitching healthy yeast into a sugary wort under sanitary conditions eventually begins this process of anaerobic respiration, resulting in tasty, bubbly, potent beer.

You might think that while fermentation is happening, your work is done. The yeast is doing its job, and you're sitting on the sofa, waiting for the process to reach a conclusion. However, you need to be as engaged with fermentation as you were with every other stage of the process. Fermentation is a critical period for your beer. You should be taking an active role in monitoring and curating the process.

This begins with how you transfer your wort into its primary fermenter.

Preparation and Transfer

At this point, you are chilling your finished wort to the fermentation temperature as stipulated in your recipe. If you're working with an ice bath or an immersion wort chiller, you will have some time to get your fermentation equipment ready. When using a counter-flow chiller, you need to have this equipment prepared by flameout. The cooling coil deposits the wort directly into the fermenting vessel.

Here is what you need to have ready as you prepare to transfer your cooled wort:

- A fermentation vessel, like a plastic bucket or a carboy/demijohn
- A tight-seal topper for your fermenter. For buckets, this is a locking lid. For carboys, it is a cap or bung
- An airlock
- A hydrometer
- A large stirring spoon/paddle, ideally slotted, meshed, or perforated
- A drinking glass or measuring cup
- Depending on your wort filtration needs, you may need a stainless steel strainer or an auto-siphon and hose

Since you will not boil the wort again, every item that comes into contact needs to be thoroughly cleaned and sanitised. Suppose rogue microbial agents end up in your cooled wort; they will remain there and multiply throughout the fermentation, priming, and bottling processes. You don't want to end up like Bigo and find yourself spitting a foul-tasting brew into the sink.

Without sounding too much like a broken record, your only means to prevent this is diligent sterilisation, either by chemical cleaners or by heat. If you need a refresher on how best to sanitise your equipment, refer back to Chapter 3, where I detail sanitation practices.

Aeration and the Pour

The physical transfer from a brew kettle to a fermenting vessel is relatively straightforward. As long as you have all your equipment ready and sterilised and your wort is cooled to the appropriate temperature to receive yeast, you can simply pour it straight into your fermenter.

Each time you move your wort from one vessel to another in brewing terms, this is known as 'racking', as I will now refer to it.

You might feel uneasy about your wort splashing around during the transfer. On the contrary, you should welcome this movement. You want your racking from brew pot to fermenter to be a little unsettling to aerate your wort. Wort aeration supplies plenty of oxygen, which initially helps the yeast to grow and reproduce, as they will be able to respire aerobically. After this point, when you have propagated a healthy active yeast culture, you will want the oxygen to run out, forcing the yeast to switch to anaerobic respiration. Then you're in business...

Although aeration is good, the transfer still needs to be a controlled pour. If you aren't careful, you could find a fermenter full of stray proteins and hops. Even worse, you might pour your tasty wort all over the floor. Not only will you lose an entire batch, but you'll also be mopping and re-mopping a sticky floor.

How you control your transfer depends on what type of tun and fermenter you're working with. Here is a handy cheat sheet to determine the best technique for racking into the fermenter:

- **From Brew Pot > Fermenting Bucket:-** you should carefully tip the cooled pot into the bucket, creating a steady waterfall of wort into the fermenter.

- **From Brew Kettle > Fermenting Bucket:-** you should position the bucket directly below your kettle spigot and start the flow.
- **From Brew Pot > Carboy:** you can position a sanitised funnel over the carboy opening and pour the wort through that. One inaccurate pour, however, and you will shower your floor in wort. A safer, more precise option is to transfer the cooled wort with an auto-siphon and hose.
- **From Brew Kettle > Carboy:** you should position the carboy opening under the kettle spigot and start the flow. For more precise pouring, attach a rubber hose to the tap.

If you are pouring directly from a pot, you need to keep your sanitised stirring spoon nearby. Ideally, at this point, you should ask your partner or a friend to spot you with the spoon, catching any hop bags and sludge that may try to escape.

Clearing Post-Brew Sediment

Remember that after flameout, you proceeded straight into wort chilling. That means lots of sediment is still floating in your brew pot when it comes time to rack. This residual material, or trub, includes:

- Hot break, proteins that coagulate in the pot/kettle during boiling
- Cold break, proteins that separate and settle during wort chilling
- Spent hops, which are lying at the bottom of your pot or kettle in a steeping bag

It is nearly impossible to separate all this residue from your wort. However, a small quantity of lingering break will not adversely affect your final beer. Conversely, if you have too much, it can lead to off-flavours or smells in the finished product.

Keeping as much sediment out of your fermenter as possible is the primary goal. A bag of wet hops can easily be removed from the pot with your sanitised spoon. However, proteins and other loose sediment are a little trickier to manage. Here are some techniques homebrewers use to prevent break material from entering the primary fermenter:

1. Place a stainless-steel strainer (sanitised, of course) over your fermenter and pour your wort slowly through it. This will catch most break residue.
2. Create a whirlpool in your cooled brew pot by stirring the wort constantly. This will force most residual sediment to the centre while you siphon wort from the perimeter.
3. Have a secondary fermentation vessel. After transferring the wort to your bucket, allow it to settle, then siphon it to a second bucket or carboy, leaving any residue in the first fermenter.

Bear in mind that some beer styles require more serious filtering than others. Suppose you are brewing a thick, impenetrable Stout or Barley wine; you might find success with a careful pour or, at most, a strainer over your bucket. Some types of beer require greater clarity—for example, Pilsners and other light Lagers.

Topping Off – As briefly mentioned in the previous chapter, most extract beer recipes call for topping off with clean water. This will dilute your concentrated wort and increase the overall batch volume. In keeping with the best practice of constant sanitation, you should make sure this water and anything holding it are sterile. You can do this by boiling the water ahead of time and then cooling it. Alternatively, you can purchase bottled water.

Give it a solid shake before adding your topping-off water to the fermenter. You want to aerate the water just like you did your wort.

Selecting and Adding Brewing Yeast

Once you have racked your wort to its fermenter, taken care to separate any trub, and topped it off with water (if needed), you are ready to pitch in your brewer's yeast.

Ale Yeast vs Lager Yeast – It will be helpful to note at this stage that the only distinction between an ale and a lager is the type of yeast used to ferment it.

Ale yeast strains are known as Saccharomyces cerevisiae. This was the original type of yeast used in brewing and is the same type used in baking. Whether the brewer knew it or not, cerevisiae was used for hundreds of years before the discovery of lager yeast. Interestingly, according to the Bavarian 'Beer Purity Law' of 1516, yeast was not named as a beer ingredient, suggesting that they knew nothing of its presence. To ancient Bavarian brewers, beer was just barley, hops, and water—albeit with a bit of 'magic' thrown in.

In terms of science, these yeast types are usually top-fermenting, meaning that as they do their work, they rise to the top of the wort. As fermentation progresses, you will see a heady yeast coating inside your carboy or bucket. Ale yeast strains do their work at higher temperatures than lager yeast strains. Their ideal range is 65-72°F (18-22°C), although they will do just fine at anything between 50 and 77°F (10-25°C). For this reason, many first-time brewers tend to favour ale styles like Pales, Porters, Stouts, Altbiers, and Kolsch.

Lager yeast strains are known as *Saccharomyces pastorianus*, after Louis Pasteur. As far as we know, this type of yeast was first spoken of in Nuremberg, Southern Germany; hence, lager is thought to be of Bavarian origin. Brewers were aware of the existence of *pastorianus* long before it was given its own taxonomical classification in 1883. Before classification, it was known as - *Saccharomyces carlsbergensis*—a name given to it in 1885 when it was donated to the Danish Carlsberg brewery by the Spaten Brewery in Berlin. This name is sometimes still referred to in the scientific literature, even though it is now incorrect.

In addition, lager yeast has a somewhat fascinating history, and modern scientists have had great difficulty tracing its exact origin. However, due to advances in genetic sequencing, it is now known that *pastorianus* is a hybrid yeast strain: a genetic mix of standard ale yeast (*Saccharomyces cerevisiae*) and *Saccharomyces eubayanus*. The latter is believed to have arrived in Europe from Patagonia, most likely along a slave route, although this can't be confirmed. There is also little evidence to suggest whether the hybridisation of the two yeast species happened in Europe, South America, or Asia. This will likely be the subject of much debate for years to come.

In terms of science, these yeast types are usually bottom-fermenting, settling on the floor of your primary fermenter. Their ideal temperature range is cooler at 44-60°F (7-15°C), a characteristic they gained from their *Saccharomyces eubayanus*-parent. Using lager yeast requires your primary fermenter to stay in a cool, climate-controlled space. One benefit of this colder process is that infection and 'off' flavours are less likely. It's little wonder that most lager styles, such as Pilsners or Oktoberfests, are considered clean, clear, and crisp.

To conclude, there are many strains of brewer's yeast, and some breweries have even developed their own "house" cultures. Each strain processes fermentable sugar at a different rate. Still, they lend additional aesthetic notes to the beer just as significantly. Yeast plays a vital role in the colour, body, flavours, and bouquet of your beer. For example, English Ale Yeast strains impart the woody, funky character that folks associate with Real Ale. Belgian Ale yeasts impart and accentuate fruity, spicy notes in the beer. Much like malt and hops, your yeast strain will be decided based on your beer type.

Brewers use two essential metrics to determine the strength and efficiency of brewer's yeast. They are:

- **Attenuation** - This measures what percentage of the fermentable sugars in wort will be converted by the yeast. A low-attenuating yeast will convert about 72%, while a high-attenuating yeast will convert 78%.
- **Flocculation** - This measures how quickly your yeast will clump, ending its activity in the wort.

Be sure to check the packaging for the brewer's yeast strain in your recipe. It will provide more detailed information about your yeast strain, including its ideal temperature range, storage instructions, attenuation, and flocculation.

Pitching Your Yeast – Before you pitch in your yeast, double-check that it is at an appropriate temperature, generally 68-72° F (20–22° C) for ales and 45-57° F (7–14° C) for lagers. It is also a good idea to immerse the closed packet or canister of yeast in a no-rinse sanitiser to ensure that no stray microbes get transferred with the yeast.

Be aware that some yeasts can be thrown in as they are, whereas others must be shaken and smacked to activate the cultures. Always read the packaging and recipe instructions to ensure you're adding your yeast correctly.

Understanding and Checking Gravity

Once your wort is racked to your primary fermenter and your yeast is added, you should retain some of the fermenting wort in a sanitised glass to check its original gravity. Original gravity (OG) is the term given to the density of the liquid wort before fermentation. For this, you will use your hydrometer.

A hydrometer essentially measures the amount of water in a liquid, hence the first part, 'hydro'. As the sugars are used up by the yeast, they will disappear, causing the density of the liquid to decrease. The resulting alcohol is much less dense than the sugars we began with, meaning your hydrometer reading should continue to fall over the fermentation period. Moreover, the degree to which this happens will let you know the alcohol content of your beer at each point.

Pure water has a specific gravity of 1. If you were to brew an English IPA, your wort's original gravity would be in the range of 1.05 to 1.075. This means that the wort is 5% to 7.5% denser than pure water. You would hope so after spending two hours pitching malt extract, milled barley, hops, and yeast into your strike water.

After one to two weeks, the IPA you brewed will end somewhere between 1.01 and 1.018. This is your final gravity (FG).

Being diligent enough to check your gravity throughout fermentation means you can anticipate when it will reach its conclusion and, therefore, when it's time to sanitise your bottles and bottle tops.

Also, by subtracting the final gravity from the original gravity, you can determine the change in density due to fermentation. For those who are adept at maths, with a simple calculation, you'll also be able to find out your beer's alcohol by volume (ABV). Here is the formula:

ABV = 132.715(OG-FG)

For your hypothetical English IPA, this calculation might read:

ABV = 132.715(1.075-1.018) = 132.715 x 0.057

ABV = approximately 7.6%

Yeast Pitching Rate

No, I'm not talking about how many times you throw your baseball towards home plate. The pitching rate is the amount of yeast you need to add to your cooled wort to convert it to fermented beer—although, let's hope you don't wind up following through after drinking it.

Without using too many toilet puns, I don't want you getting bogged down with calculations at this stage. However, it is helpful to note that if you make an ale of standard ABV (around 5%-6%), your pitching rate is about 6 million yeast cells per millilitre of wort. If you're brewing a five-gallon batch, this works out to roughly 113.5 billion cells. Lagers tend to have about double the pitching rate of ales.

Pitching Rate and your Beer Profile - A lower pitching rate will require the yeast to be in contact with the wort for longer. This means it will impart more flavour notes on the finished beer. Consider beers with prominent yeast notes: Abbey Ales, Ole Ales, and ESBs, to name a few. All these beers tend to have lower pitching rates.

Finding a healthy medium for yeast pitching is critical. The finished beer's flavour profile might be overtaken with fruity esters if you under-pitch. If you overpitch, you could ferment more sugars than you intended, leading to off-flavours and a final gravity outside of your target beer style.

Another factor that may affect your beer's pitching rate is fermentation temperature and original gravity.

The environmental impact of colder lager fermentation will significantly increase a recipe's pitching rate since cold slows down cellular respiration. Regarding original gravity, denser wort puts pressure on cells, slowing the fermentation process. Additionally, as fermentation progresses, a wort with an OG above 1.06 will have lots of ethyl alcohol. This also inhibits yeast metabolism.

So, for both cold fermentation and high-OG worts, you will need to compensate with more yeast cells, resulting in the need for a higher pitching rate. You might also need to jump-start the process using a yeast starter.

Making A Yeast Starter – Essentially, a starter gets your yeast cells working and propagating before pitching them into your wort. You need to begin making a yeast starter at least 48 hours before the boil. To make a yeast starter, you would do the following:

1. Mix 3.5 ounces (100g) of DME and 1 litre of water
2. Boil this mixture for 20 minutes
3. Cool the starter wort to 70 °F (21 °C)
4. Transfer the cooled starter to a sanitised mason jar
5. Add your yeast and cover loosely with sanitised aluminium foil or a sanitised lid

6. Swirl the mixture to agitate your yeast cells
7. Agitate the start periodically over the next two days
8. Pitch the entire mix in your cool wort to begin fermentation

Your yeast will be pre-measured if you're working with a packaged beer kit. As bought from a brew store, most yeast starter packs will contain the correct 6 million yeast cells per millilitre of wort once pitched into a 5-gallon batch. You won't need to worry about pitching rate or starter cultures. Just make sure that you follow the instructions on your yeast package.

If you are crafting your own recipe, it's best to triple-check your pitching rate. Wyeast has an excellent Pitch Rate Calculator on their company website. I also recommend you talk to your local brewing supply retailer. Workers at these establishments know their products, and they tend to be avid homebrewers themselves.

There will be more detailed information on making starter cultures, specific gravity measurements, and pitching rate calculations in *Beer Brewing Bliss: All-Grain Brewing Mastery*.

Sealing and Stowing for Fermentation

Once your wort is racked, and you've pitched your yeast, it's time to seal your vessel for fermentation. If you have a carboy, secure its bung or cap. If you're using a fermentation bucket, seal its lid tightly. Most importantly, affix your airlock to the fermenter's opening. The airlock will protect the wort from outside infiltration, allow carbon dioxide to escape, and provide a visual aid to show how fermentation is progressing. Not much in life is as satisfying as seeing the bobber on your airlock bouncing up and down! I said, "not much"...

Stowing your Fermenter – You should avoid two things at all costs when storing your fermenter: temperature fluctuation and UV light.

I have already discussed how brewer's yeast works best within specific temperature ranges. Make sure your fermenter is stored in a location that will remain within that range. If you're working with lager yeast, you might find that a spare refrigerator is your best fermenting space.

Your fermenter's location should also be away from sunlight. Prolonged exposure to UV rays, whether during fermentation or bottling, will encourage off-flavours and inhibit yeast growth. Keeping fermenters away from direct sunlight is particularly important when using glass carboys, as they are fully transparent. They must be stowed in as dark a location as possible. If you're using a white bucket, the area can afford to be moderately dark.

You should generally look for a secluded area that doesn't get hot in the middle of the day or is incredibly cold at night. Founders Brewing in Michigan store their KBS (a beloved Barrel-Aged Stout) in an underground cavern system for a year prior to bottling. Like Joan of Arc's 800-year-old rain water, you probably don't have a dark cave nearby. If you did, life would probably be far more bearable. A cellar or interior closet will do the job perfectly in both cases.

The Fermentation Timeline – The interaction between yeast and wort is a little different for every beer. However, all fermentation follows a three-stage process. Here's a general breakdown of how your wort ferments:

- **Lag Phase** - 3-15 Hours. The yeast adjusts to its new environment. They bolster their structure with amino acids, vitamins, minerals, and oxygen from the wort.
- **Exponential Growth Phase** - 1-4 Days. Yeast cells rapidly increase, processing sugars as they grow. They process glucose, sucrose, and fructose first, creating ethanol and carbon dioxide. Then, yeast process maltose and maltotriose, which contribute primarily to flavour and body. During this phase, your airlock will percolate like crazy, and a thick brown foam will form on top of the wort.
- **Stationary Phase** - 3- 10 Days. Yeast slows down, and your beer begins to mature. Estery compounds get reabsorbed by the yeast. Sulphurous gas escapes. Soon, the yeast starts settling in a cake at the bottom of the fermenter.

During fermentation, you will continue taking hydrometer readings. Suppose you want to avoid constantly opening your fermenter and disturbing your wort. In this case, you can maintain a 'satellite fermenter' during this time. Hold onto the wort you drew for your starting gravity reading (ensuring that it's not taken until the yeast has been pitched). Store it in a sanitised bottle with a clean paper towel secured with an elastic band as the stopper. You can keep this satellite fermenter in the dark cabinet, out of the way.

The wort inside the bottle will serve as a concurrently fermenting sample for gravity readings over the coming weeks.

Secondary Fermentation and Lagering

You might have noticed that I occasionally refer to primary fermenters. Some brewers will rack their wort to a secondary fermenter, either a second bucket or carboy.

For some beer styles, secondary fermentation is compulsory. For most ales, it is optional and often unnecessary. Here are some of the reasons a brewer might want to rack to a secondary fermenter:

- As stated earlier, racking to a second fermenter can help filter out more of the hot break and cold break sediment.
- Lagers and low-gravity ales require a rest period to clarify and slough off fermentation by-products. A secondary fermenter is often the best place for this rest period.
- Once your wort nears the final phase of fermentation, a secondary fermenter can be a cleaner environment for it to attenuate in
- High-gravity beers sometimes need to age longer before priming and bottling. Separating them from yeast in a second fermenter can prevent unwanted by-product infiltration.
- A secondary fermenter can provide a clean vessel for flavour additions like dry hops, fruit, coffee, or wood.

For the most part, racking to a secondary fermenter is not necessary to yield a quality final beer. Unless your recipe says you need a secondary fermenter, you can go straight from fermentation to priming and bottling.

The Lagering Process – Despite its name, lagering can be done with any style of beer. It is simply a process of ageing in a secondary fermenter at cold temperatures. The end goal of lagering is obtaining a clean-tasting beer devoid of turbidity or sediment.

Due to its origins in Bavaria, lagering gets its name from the German word '*lagern*', which means 'to store'. This process has been carried out in Germany and Austria for hundreds of years. Still, lagering didn't take hold across the rest of the world until the latter part of the 19th century. The industrial revolution brought advances in refrigeration and the ability to isolate pure yeast strains, making the process much more accessible—particularly to those who lived in parts of the world where cold temperatures were difficult to maintain.

Today, lagered beers, including the traditional lagers 'Pilsner' and 'Bock', account for more than 90% of the beer produced worldwide. Once you have the correct equipment (and by that, I mean a large refrigerator), the process of lagering is actually a pretty simple one.

After fermentation is complete, the primary fermenter is removed from its cool environment and allowed to increase to room temperature. This is called a diacetyl rest. Diacetyl is a compound created by some yeast strains that cause buttery flavours. Diacetyl is no big deal in small amounts and in big robust beers. However, it can create an unpleasant taste in light, crisp lagers. Two to three days of rest allows the compound to settle out of the wort.

Brewers rack to a secondary fermenter and let the beer age at a temperature just above freezing. This is the actual lagering phase. During this time, which can last anywhere from 10 days to over a month, sulphuric odours dissipate, and residual sediment falls off. The beer should be crystalline and refreshing at the end of lagering, with just enough yeast hanging on to allow natural carbonation.

Because it involves cold fermentation and additional ageing, the lagering process takes much longer to finish than standard ale fermentation. Altogether, you might spend nearly two months on a single batch of lager instead of a couple of weeks for the average ale. If you're brewing your first batch, I strongly recommend avoiding a recipe that requires lagering.

That's all for now on fermentation. You have the necessary information and skills to confidently pitch yeast into your extract batch. Beer Brewing Bliss: All-Grain Brewing Mastery will give more information and tips on diacetyl rest and the lagering process.

Chapter Six

Priming

After fermentation, your wort can finally be called beer. Fully attenuated and bursting with flavour, it would taste just about finished if you siphoned a glass from the fermenter. However, there would be one major component missing: carbonation. You need to prime before you can seal your delicious homebrewed beer in bottles. Let's get into this quick but essential stage in the beer-making process.

Ensuring Fermentation Has Ended

Before you rack your beer for priming and bottling, you must be sure that fermentation has concluded. The result can be somewhat disappointing if your yeast cells are still working through fermentable sugars when adding priming sugar and enclosing it in bottles. At best, you will have off-flavours and gushing upon opening. At worst, your bottles will explode during the carbonation process.

The unmistakable sign that fermentation is finished is that your beer's gravity has not changed in several days. Getting a similar value on multiple hydrometer readings is enough to ensure that the fermentable material has been used up. During the lag and exponential growth phases of fermentation (i.e., the first five days), you will not need to measure the gravity of your wort. Any reading during those phases would be effectively meaningless since it would be measuring a point on a rapidly moving target.

However, midway through the second week of fermentation on an average-strength ale, you should start taking hydrometer readings every couple of days. Once the wort reaches the final gravity window for your recipe, begin taking readings daily. After three days of unchanged specific gravity, you can be reasonably confident that fermentation is done.

Remember that your yeast starter 'smack pack' will probably include instructions on how long your beer should stay in its primary fermenter. While this isn't gospel for every beer, it's a valuable benchmark. You can usually wait until the end of the fermenting window indicated on your yeast packaging, then take your first hydrometer reading.

In addition, the specifics of your wort recipe might affect the required fermentation time. Instructions on the yeast pack may state that your wort will be finished in two weeks. Still, it may not account for a higher original gravity or a low fermenting temperature. Both of these factors can extend the fermenting timeline significantly. You can only be sure if you take regular hydrometer readings.

Remember that your original and final gravity readings will be predetermined in extract brewing. Your malt extract and steeping grains are pre-portioned, as is your brewer's yeast. The recipe and instructions you're following will also provide a fermentation timeline. You will unlikely see an unexpectedly longer or shorter fermentation if you follow your brewing instructions correctly.

In the next book, Beer Brewing Bliss: All-Grain Brewing Mastery, I will discuss the many variables associated with a beer's gravity.

Preparation and Bottling

If this is your first time as a homebrewer, you might be shocked by what you find in your primary fermenter when it's time to prime and bottle. Of course, I'm not talking about a silk nightgown or smoking pipe.

For a standard-strength ale, you can expect to see some residual foam (known as krausen, from the German word for 'curly') on top of your wort. You will also see some crusted by-products along the sides of your fermenting vessel. At the bottom sits the dense trub, or 'yeast cake'. As outlined in the last chapter, these are the many remnants of the fermenting process. Yeast cake would be a terrible accompaniment to your morning tea, and you also don't want it anywhere near your final bottled beer.

Consequently, when preparing to prime your fermented wort, you should avoid disturbing these by-products. Whether racking from the fermenter into a bottling bucket or into bottles, you should stay clear of your fermenter's top, bottom, and sides when submerging your siphon.

Bottling Straight from the Fermenter - Before outlining the pros and cons of bottling straight from your fermenting vessel, I will first urge caution. This process is tricky and isn't something you should consider unless you have a brewing partner or friend on standby. Siphoning from a bucket or carboy into a bottle requires more skill and attention than one person can manage comfortably.

Let me break down the Scylla and Charybdis of bottling from the fermenter.

Firstly, to avoid trub and other residues in your fermenter, you must submerge your sanitised auto-siphon about four inches into the finished wort. Keeping a stabilising hand on the racking cane, give the siphon a couple of solid pumps. The flow should be even and stable without any bubbles or sediment. Slowly lower your siphon as the volume of liquid in the fermenter decreases. You should also keep an eye on the hose, as once the beer flow becomes clouded, you know you've reached the trub, and it's time to stop siphoning.

Secondly, you want to avoid adding any air during this process. Aeration was good when racking from your brew kettle to your fermenter but is best avoided after fermentation has ended. Oxygen helps your yeast grow during the lag phase of fermentation. Still, in the finished beer, such oxidation can cause cardboard-like flavours. To prevent air infiltration, make sure the end of your auto-siphon doesn't accidentally emerge from the wort during bottling. Also, you should keep the end of the hose near the bottom of your bottles or use a bottling wand to prevent splashing.

When racking straight to bottles, there are many factors to consider and the potential for things to go wrong. I would therefore advise that the novice homebrewer avoid this method like Pasteur's plague — at least for now.

Racking to a Bottling Bucket - It may take a little longer to rack your fermented wort from the fermenter to a bottling bucket before you prime and bottle. Although this extra step solves a lot of logistical problems and will prevent you from ruining a lot of hard work.

Firstly, you won't have to juggle bottles in one hand with a siphon and hose in the other. Even if you have a competent helper, there will likely still be spillages and waste when bottling straight from the fermenter. You can now lay the end of your siphon hose on the bucket floor and dedicate all your focus to positioning the racking cane away from air and trub. This is also a much better option for the introvert brewer, as you won't have to make idle conversation with anyone else.

Since your hose fills the bottling bucket from the bottom, there will be no splashing to oxidise your beer. This also provides an additional layer of protection for your beer. There is also another advantage to using a bottling bucket. Even if some loose sediment does find its way into the bucket, it will have time to settle out below the spigot before you begin bottling.

Finally, the bottling bucket is the ideal place to add your priming sugar, bringing us nicely to the priming process itself.

Adding your Primer

Even though your brewer's yeast has finished fermenting sugars and attenuating your wort, it isn't completely done with its work. You may have racked to a secondary fermenter, done a diacetyl rest, lagered the wort for weeks, and then racked again. However, plenty of active yeast cells remain in the finished product.

The priming process involves feeding those leftover yeast cells the additional sugars needed to produce carbon dioxide gas inside the bottle. Adding carbonation to beer in such a way is known as bottle conditioning. This is the only natural way for the homebrewer to achieve carbonation without having industrial equipment or a keg.

The commercial alternative to bottle conditioning is forced carbonation. Large breweries can pump carbon dioxide through their beer in a sealed container, carbonating it over time. I will discuss this process in a little more detail in the next book, but for now, let's focus on bottle conditioning, as this is what you will most likely be doing.

Priming with Sugar - The most common sugars used for priming are cane and corn sugar. These products are preferred because they do their work without noticeably altering the beer's flavour. You can also use brown sugar, maple sugar, candi sugar, DME, or other fermentable sugars to tweak or intensify specific flavour notes in your brew.

To prime your beer with cane or corn sugar, you will first need to dissolve the sugar in boiling water. Your goal is to have enough water to dissolve the sugar without affecting the overall batch volume. You will want about 2 cups of water for every 4-5 oz (115-140g) of corn sugar or 3.8-4.8 oz (110-135g) of cane sugar. Dissolving your sugar in boiling water only makes it easier to blend in with the beer, so don't worry if the water volume is not exact.

Once your priming sugar has fully dissolved, I recommend letting it cool before adding it to your sanitised bottling bucket. Make sure you cover the mixture whilst cooling to prevent the entry of bacteria. You will also want to protect your bottling bucket. Alternatively, some brewers prefer to add dissolved priming sugar directly to the primary fermenter. They argue that once the sugar is in the finished wort, siphoning either into a bucket or your bottles creates natural cycling that effectively distributes the sugars.

In my opinion, the risks of adding priming sugar to your fermenter outweigh any potential benefits.

Firstly, pouring a hot sugary addition to the finished wort will disturb trub and other by-products you want to keep out of your beer bottles. Additionally, this method requires you to estimate how much sugar you need. As I will discuss shortly, calculating your priming needs begins with knowing the exact quantity of wort you will be bottling. Once added to the bottling bucket, you will know exactly how much beer you have. Only then can you determine how much priming sugar you should use.

Secondly, racking to a bottling bucket separates your liquid from the dense yeast cake at the bottom of your fermenter.

I recommend adding your priming solution to your bottling bucket instead of your primary fermenter for these two reasons.

Priming with Tablets - There is another option for bottle conditioning your beer. This option might prove infinitely more attractive if you are siphoning directly from your fermenting vessel into bottles or if you don't have a bottling bucket.

Priming tablets, also known as carbonation drops, are small capsules of hard corn or cane sugar. You simply drop these tablets directly into each bottle, then fill the bottles with fermented wort. Once each bottle is sealed, the residual yeast begins working on the sugars, creating carbon dioxide gas. After about a week, the priming tablet will be fully dissolved. Because the bottle is capped, no carbonation will escape until you open it, giving that satisfying hissing sound when you finally crack it open.

Carbonation drops do offer some advantages over racking to a bottling bucket, such as:

- They take much less time to pitch in and involve no additional equipment

- They are pre-portioned to the amount of beer going into your bottle
- One package can be used across multiple batches
- You can avoid over-priming, which may lead to unexpected explosions

There are, however, two potential pitfalls of using priming tablets.

Firstly, they are more expensive than priming sugar. Remember, time is money. A bag of 60 carbonation caps costs $6 (£4) instead of approximately $2.50 (£2) for an equivalent amount of priming sugar. Of course, this increase in cost might be worth it for the ease of use, especially if you're bottling directly from your primary fermenter.

Secondly, the amount of priming sugar you need for your batch is dependent on the temperature and style of your beer. Depending on the type of beer you're making, and if you mess with your recipe, a full tab might over-carbonate your bottle. Many homebrewers smash these tabs with a hammer and divide one tablet across two bottles.

At this point, you may think, "Surely that defeats the point!" Sure, priming tabs are designed to make life easier. Still, sadly a 'one size fits all' approach doesn't usually apply to brewing due to its many variables. If you are using an extract recipe, you should be OK with priming tabs, although, for the all-grain brewer, it may end up being more trouble than it's worth.

The factors affecting the pitching of priming sugar will be discussed in more detail in the next book. You know the name...

Effect of Priming on ABV - After learning the science of fermentation, you should wonder, "If I'm adding more sugar to my finished beer, won't that increase the alcohol content?"

The interaction of yeast and priming sugar will create additional ethanol and carbon dioxide; however, this alcohol increase tends to be marginal and never exceeds an extra 0.2% ABV.

This slight increase is due to all brewing yeast having an 'attenuation' limit. Yeast cells cannot consume all the sugars given after a certain period, particularly without oxygen. Due to this limited activity, you only get a small amount of additional ethanol and CO_2 produced. It is good that bottle conditioning and carbonation are controlled processes. If yeast were able to attenuate infinitely, you would end up with thin, tasteless, carbonated, alcoholic water.

Factors Affecting Measurement – Beer recipes are like snowflakes: no two are exactly alike. You can group them into styles and substyles, but in the end, each beer is unique to itself.

In my time, I have enjoyed Blonde Stouts, Black IPAs, Pastry Sours, Imperial Lagers, and Wild-Fermented Baltic Porters. There is no such thing as a standard recipe, and as such, each priming measurement will also be completely unique. Here are the factors you need to consider when setting a priming sugar weight for your batch:

- **Batch size** - As the volume of liquid increases, so does the amount of priming sugar.
- **Temperature** - The colder your fermented wort is out of the fermenter, the more carbonation has built up in the liquid. You need to account for this existing carbonation.

- **Sugar Type** - Different priming sugars affect the flavour of the finished beer differently. They also yield carbon dioxide at different rates.
- **Desired Carbonation Volumes** - You can decide how effervescent you want your finished beer to be. Each beer style has a range of carbon dioxide volume that is standard. For example, a fizzy, refreshing Lager would reside in a carbonation window of 2.2-2.7 volumes, while a more tepid English Ale would be in the 1.3-2.3 range. More information on CO_2 volumes will be given in the next book.

With so many variables to consider, we are lucky that online tools already exist to perform the necessary calculations for us.

I personally use the free calculator available on the website 'Brewer's Friend' for my priming needs. You can enter your batch size, temperature, and desired carbonation volumes here. The calculator then gives accurate measures for all 17 most common priming sugars. You can then rest assured that whatever you are priming will be correct, provided you measure it out accurately.

So, which option is best for you?

For anyone just starting out, I recommend taking the path of least resistance. Don't learn to drive 'off road', so to speak. If you have one, use a bottling bucket - your batch recipe may include a pre-measured bag of priming sugar. The recipe will also consist of boiling and pitching instructions. Later, there is plenty of time to experiment with different priming sugars and CO_2 levels when you progress to all-grain brewing.

If you don't have a bottling bucket, I suggest you purchase a bag of priming tablets. Sixty tabs should be more than enough for a five-gallon extract batch. If you are brewing a middle-strength ale, the sugar contained in each capsule should be just about suitable for a 12-ounce bottle. You can add one tablet per sanitised bottle and fill it with confidence.

Chapter Seven

Bottling and Storage

Now you're on the home stretch, with your wort fully fermented, attenuated, and primed. All that's left is to pour it into your bottles and seal it!

The bottle is where your beer will reach full maturity. It's where beer gains carbonation and where its flavours develop and adhere. When you pop open that bottle in a few weeks, what comes out will be your beer, start to finish. You should be proud of what you have achieved.

But there are still some pivotal steps ahead. As Han Solo would say, "Don't get cocky, kid."

Filling and Capping

At this point in the process, you will need the following equipment:

- A bottling bucket with a spigot, if you aren't bottling directly from your primary fermenter
- A siphon and hose if you are bottling from the primary fermenter
- Enough bottles to contain your entire batch (approximately 48 per 5-gallon)
- Caps, if you are working with standard long-neck bottles
- A bottle capper, if you are working with standard long-neck bottles
- A pot or tub to catch any spilt beer

A bottle filler stick (or wand) attachment is beneficial when filling from a bottling bucket. This plastic wand attaches to your bucket's spigot. It releases beer only when its stopper is depressed on the bottom of a bottle. This attachment regulates beer flow and prevents oxidation by filling bottles from the bottom; it also makes the process much simpler by removing the need to stop and start your spigot with each fill. Magic!

Sanitising for Bottling - Just as the bottle is the final container your beer goes through before consumption, it is also the last place where it can be ruined. Remember, out of the fermenter, your beer should never touch anything that has not been thoroughly sanitised. This means that your bottling equipment and containers must be cleaned and either rinsed in a sanitising solution or exposed to a sterilising heat level.

If you aren't sick of hearing about sanitation and need a refresher, please refer to Chapter 3, where I covered this subject.

Suppose you don't opt for the refresher; I do want to offer a few bottling-specific sanitising tips before we move on to the filling process:

- Sanitising bottles with a chemical solution like StarSan and PBW can be laborious and time-consuming but necessary. I recommend filling a big tub or bucket with sanitiser and submerging as many bottles as possible.
- Alternatively, you can run these bottles through a dishwasher boil cycle with no detergent.
- The neck and interior of the bottles are the most critical areas to keep microbe-free. It is best to handle sanitised bottles as you would at the bar, grabbing them around the base.
- A few lingering droplets of no-rinse sanitising solution in your bottle are fine, but you don't want to leave lots of liquid there. You can purchase a handy bottle-drying tree that efficiently positions bottles to drain off sanitiser. These products cost about $25-$30 (£20). Obviously, you want to clean and sanitise your drying tree before each use.
- Your bottle caps also need to be sterile. I recommend placing them in a bowl of sanitising solution and pulling them out as required for capping.

- You should keep your bottle capper clean, but you don't need to sanitise it. It only comes in contact with the outside of your bottle and cap, not your beer.

Bottling from the Fermenting Vessel - If you ditch the bottling bucket altogether, you will need to use your siphon and tubing to draw finished wort directly into your bottles. To do this, you should have all bottles sanitised, dried, and lined up for filling. You should also have a bucket or tub ready to catch any split beer. This will happen with this method.

Once you have a good flow going through your siphon, place the end of the hose at the bottom of the bottle and fill until about the beer reaches 3/4 inch from the top. This will allow room to accommodate the carbon dioxide released during bottle conditioning. Once you get the desired fill level, squeeze the tubing to stop the beer flow, then move on to the next bottle.

Personally, I can only rack directly from fermenter to bottle with a second pair of hands. Bear in mind that if you go down this road, you will be working with a siphon inside wort which contains trub and other sediment. You will also be dealing with a steady flow of liquid while juggling 48 bottles. I'm going to assume that you're not a professional court jester, so I strongly recommend you also have a bottling partner.

You also may want to look back to Chapter 6 before bottling from your primary fermenter. This chapter meticulously covers the pros and pitfalls of racking fermented wort. Here is a quick summary of three main factors that you need to account for:

1. Your fermenter will have by-product crusting the edges, and the wort will have a foamy residue called krausen on top. Avoid siphoning this into bottles by placing your racking cane 3-4 inches into the centre of the wort before siphoning.
2. Your yeast will have collected in a cake at the bottom of the fermenter. You should avoid racking this into your bottle by your siphon before it reaches the fermenter's floor.
3. Aeration is undesirable at this point and will cause off-flavours in your finished beer. To

avoid oxygen infiltration, keep your racking cane submerged in your wort until the end.

Finally, the best way to prime your finished wort if you don't have a bottling bucket is to drop a priming tablet (or carbonation drop) into each bottle.

Bottling from a Bucket - Once you have racked your fermented wort from the fermenter to a bottling bucket and primed it with sugar (if you aren't using carbonation drops), you can start filling bottles.

To begin, you might need to reposition your bottling bucket after racking. You must position it low to the floor to allow gravity to help your siphoning. Once your bucket is full, you need it higher and near the edge of a counter or table to open the spigot above the bottle. Make this move gingerly to prevent sloshing. When pouring your wort into the bottle from a spout, it is better to tilt it as if you were pulling a pint of beer from a tap. Anyone who's been a barman/woman before will have had plenty of practice at this.

Again, I strongly recommend you purchase a bottle filling wand. It is incredibly affordable ($8-$12 or £5) and makes filling bottles a breeze. Suppose you don't have a bottle filler attachment for your bottling bucket; you can attach a short length of sanitised tubing to the fixture. The idea is obviously to limit the number of oxidising splashes during filling. A one-foot length of hose will release liquid at the floor of each bottle, filling it from the bottom.

As with bottling directly from the fermenter, you want to leave 3/4 inch of space with each fill.

Capping - If you are conditioning your beer in glass swing-top bottles or PET plastic bottles, you can seal them off by hand. If you are using long-neck glass bottles, you will need a capper.

It doesn't matter whether you cap as you fill or affix caps all at once at the end. What matters at this point is that your capping is tight and secure. If your beer undergoes bottle-conditioning with loose or ill-fitted caps, carbon dioxide may leak out, and oxygen may leak in. In the end, you could have a flat, stale-tasting beer.

Whether you are using a hand capper or a bench capper, always place the cap centrally on the head of your bottle and cinch it to the capper's full motion. If the cap seems loose, pop it off and try again. Better to lose a twenty-cent cap than a whole bottle of homebrew.

Storing Your Bottles

You should always stow your conditioning bottles using the same criteria you used for fermentation. Find a place that is free of direct sunlight or significant temperature fluctuations. You want the yeast working on the priming sugar to be far from UV rays and extreme heat or cold. For a mid-range ale, the temperature should stay around 65-75°F (18-23°C). You can refer to Chapter 5 about fermentation for more details about ideal storage temperatures for each beer type.

If your bottles come with a wooden crate or cardboard box, you can return them to these containers before storing them. I also recommend placing paper towels underneath your conditioning bottles. Lining your bottle box with paper will absorb most of the mess, and clean up will be minimal.

Conditioning - If we think about bottle conditioning in purely practical terms, the process is about getting carbon dioxide into beer. Still, bottle conditioning is about so much more than carbonation. It is essential to establish a beer's unique, matured character.

Consider the Trappist Ale. These official monastery beers, normally high-ABV and dark, are almost always bottle conditioned. The methods monks use to bottle beer with just the right amount of residual Belgian Ale yeast and prime it with candi sugar create the inimitable fruity fullness and slight funk that we associate with abbey beer.

Conditioning is not limited to bottles either. Gravity-pumped Real Ale is delivered to English pubs with the yeast still doing their work. The continuous process of sugar conversion into carbon dioxide gives this ale its green, musty flavours.

A conditioned beer is alive in the truest sense. In some ales, yeast will continue to work within the bottle for years, allowing the taste to mature and develop.

The same is true of the beer you pour into bottles at home and cap by hand. The malt and hops you use, the type of brewer's yeast that ferments it, the time and temperature involved, and the volume of carbonation you impart add to the style of beer you have made.

The bottle is a sealed space where the final chemical processes occur, and everything comes together.

How Long to Condition in the Bottle - Your beer will need to remain in the bottle for at least two weeks. Suppose you consider that the ideal conditioning temperature for your beer is similar to your fermentation temperature; you can see why the exact bottle conditioning time frame changes from style to style and recipe to recipe.

An average strength pale ale can condition at room temperature, which means that the yeast and priming sugar have finished interacting in 2-4 weeks.

When conditioning a lager, you will keep the bottles chilled just as the fermenter was. As a result of this low temperature, the yeast will work slower, and conditioning might not be finished for up to 12 weeks.

Belgian ales are highly carbonated, traditionally. Some Trappist brews like Orval and Westmalle have carbonation volumes of 4.0-5.0, double the range of other ales. Such beers must be left to condition for 3-6 months.

If you are working from a packaged beer kit, the instructions will tell you how long your bottles need to condition before you can enjoy them. You might also consider packaging your first beer in PET plastic bottles with screw tops. You can determine if your beer has been conditioned fully by squeezing them. They are likely sufficiently carbonated if they have as much resistance as a soda bottle from the supermarket.

Once your beer has finished its bottle conditioning period, you can move bottles into the fridge and allow them to chill next to your store-bought suds.

Bottling vs Kegging

While bottling is far and away the most common way to package and condition homemade beer, it is certainly not the only option. Many homebrewers eschew bottles altogether in favour of kegs. Racking your finished beer from a primary fermenter to a 5-gallon keg has plenty of advantages. Still, it may not be the best option for novice homebrewers.

The Kegging Process – Most at-home beer makers opt to buy (or borrow) a refurbished 5-gallon (19 L) stainless steel soda keg. Depending on the manufacturer, these kegs can have different hardware and fittings, so adapters may be necessary.

Kegging also requires a carbon dioxide tank and CO_2 regulator. Brewers add carbon dioxide to the keg before racking their beer to prevent oxidation. Once the keg is full of CO_2, beer can be siphoned in through the open lid. The racking is finished by purging the keg of oxygen. Brewers do this by pumping in more CO_2 and releasing pressure repeatedly until the keg is free of oxygen.

Brewers can then increase CO_2 pressure to an appropriate level to force carbonation into the kegged beer using a relatively simple calculation. Once the right level is reached, the beer will be fully carbonated and ready to serve.

Of course, serving from a keg requires more equipment, including a tap and hosing.

You have likely noticed that kegging your homebrewed beer can be expensive. The necessary equipment will probably cost you anywhere from $120-$200 (£90-£150). That is six to ten times the cost of bottling! Alternatively, you may get away with little or even no expense if you know someone in the pub trade who has some old equipment you can borrow. They may also be able to help you with setting everything up correctly.

Pros and Cons of Kegging – Before thoroughly breaking down the advantages and disadvantages of kegs compared to bottles, I will acknowledge the innate appeal of tapping a keg of your own beer, possibly with a custom tap handle in your home bar. The idea of pouring some frosty homemade pints for your buddies is quite exciting. However, there are also significant downsides to kegging.

- **Pros** - You only need to wash and sanitise one keg instead of multiple bottles and caps. There is no need to prime with sugar since kegs are force-carbonated, which means a lower chance of oxidation or spoilage. Packaging and carbonation take very little time.
- **Cons** - A huge up-front cash expenditure, which only evens out after six to ten batches. Kegs are much more difficult to cool than bottles. Kegging equipment also requires a lot of care and upkeep.

Kegging homemade beer might be your long-term goal, which is fantastic, but I wouldn't recommend doing it too early on in your brewing days. I suggest getting a few batches under your belt before biting the bullet and buying an expensive kegging kit. There will be plenty more on kegging in the next book, *Beer Brewing Bliss: All-grain Brewing Mastery*.

That said, I have veteran homebrewer friends who vowed never to use bottles again after their first 'kegging' many moons ago. For me, this is a matter of personal preference, and I feel that both methods have their merits. In the words of Fleetwood Mac, "You can go your own way".

Chapter Eight

Top 10 Tips for a Sensational Extract Brew

Congratulations on reaching the first milestone in your brewing journey! You have now been through the entire process of making your first malt extract brew: from securing the best equipment and ingredients to the cooking, fermenting, bottling, and conditioning of your beer. You should now be just about ready to set down this book and put theory into practice. After all, practice makes perfect.

However, I am aware that there's been a lot of information to process from the preceding chapters. So before you run headlong into the wild world of homebrewing, let's review some of the best practices and explore ways to ensure you get the best quality from your beer.

1. Maintain Good Sanitary Conditions Throughout

A recurring theme of this book has been sanitary conditions, and I make no apology for it. You must ensure that everything that touches your finished wort is entirely pure and free of rogue bacteria.

Here are some important takeaways from the sanitation process.

Remember the Flame-Out Rule - Near the end of your brew day, you will boil your wort for an hour to ninety minutes. This happens, generally, while you are adding in your hops. Every tool you use up until the boil must be clean but does not need to be thoroughly sanitised. This is because boiling the wort will kill any bacteria or other harmful agents that might have entered up to that point.

However, from the moment you kill the flame on your boiling wort until the moment you open your finished beer to drink it, every surface it touches and every item that touches it must be thoroughly sanitised. Otherwise, you risk infecting your beer, gushing bottles and a foul-tasting brew.

Washing Up Tips - Every item and container you use should be cleaned before and after. Remember, no leaving dishes to go mouldy like in your student flat.

Wash every item until it is spotless, using hot water and washing up liquid. Sponges and bottle brushes are great. Heavy scouring tools are not good because they leave minor scratches and abrasions where bacteria can gather and propagate, particularly in plastics.

Sanitising with Heat - Any glass or metal tool you use in beer making can be sanitised with heat. Using heat instead of chemical agents is a better option in many ways. You don't need to worry about rinsing or drying. Heat can also reach small crevices and abrasions where liquid sanitisers might not. Here are a few options that work well:

- Pressure cookers and autoclaves ran at 257°F (125°C) for twenty minutes
- Dishwashers ran on a hot cycle without detergent
- Ovens heated at 338°F (170°C) for one hour or at 248°F (120°C) overnight

Again, sanitising with heat is a good option for metal or glass equipment, but bear in mind that plastic items may melt or become deformed. If you use heat on glass, ensure you let the things cool gradually. If you immediately expose them to cold water or freezing conditions, they may crack or shatter.

Sanitising with Chemicals - If you don't want to sanitise your beer-making tools with heat, there are many great chemical options available, including:

- Household bleach - Heavily diluted and rinsed off afterwards will kill bacteria effectively.

- StarSan/ChemSan - An excellent no-rinse liquid sanitiser with no scent or taste
- PBW and VWP - These are no-rinse granulated sanitisers. This product is almost undetectable and safe if ingested in small amounts when mixed with warm water.
- OxiClean and Other Percarbonate Cleansers - Quite effective, leaving no taste or smell. This option does require rinsing.
- Iodophor - This excellent iodine-based sanitiser is no-rinse and works with cold water. However, it can cause superficial discolouration of equipment.

Of the options listed above, my personal favourite is PBW because you can leave residual droplets behind without affecting the taste and smell of the beer. It also won't make you sick.

Rinsing and Topping-Off With Water - If your sanitising practices require rinsing with water, you should boil the water beforehand and let it cool. This will ensure you do not introduce unwanted microbes during rinsing. The same is true for water added to top off the wort after boiling. Boil it the day before and store it in the fridge in a sanitised container.

2. Use the Freshest Ingredients

Because your malt comes in extract form doesn't mean that you should settle for past-their-prime ingredients. If you pay close attention to packaging dates, your finished beer will taste the same as one made with freshly milled grain. Below is what you need to know about freshness in extract home brewing.

Liquid malt will darken and develop stale flavours within a few months due to water loss. Remember, LME is effectively wort with most of the water evaporated. As further water evaporates over time, the product becomes more concentrated. This will compound the usual issue of flavours fading over time.

Dry malt extract can last up to 8 months from the packaging without significantly reducing quality. If you are purchasing malt for a brew date that is more than two months in the future, always purchase DME if possible.

Pre-packaged speciality grains should never be more than a month old. When stored in a refrigerator, Hop pellets will stay fresh for two to four years. However, whole hops will not remain fresh for longer than a year, even when refrigerated.

If you are lucky enough to live near a homebrewing supply shop, I strongly recommend taking advantage of their services. A good brewer's supplier will have a wide selection of hops in climate-controlled conditions and fresh grain served by the pound. Their malt extracts should be cycled for freshness.

If you don't live near such an establishment, pay close attention to the packaging dates on the items you order online. Don't be afraid to ask for replacements for stale ingredients.

3. Use Good Brewing Water

As we discussed, water is the most significant component in beer, so you should pay close attention to the quality of your strike water.

Remember that the best strike water is moderately hard and has a pH that will work well with your malt bill. Since you're using an extract malt, there will already be a level of hardness imparted by the minerals in your LME or DME.

Consequently, you should mainly consider the purity of the water you use. If you live in an area with clean, soft water that is not overly alkaline, you can use your tap water. With the kit I suggested earlier, you can give it a quick hardness and pH test before using it.

Suppose you find that your tap water is overly hard, overly alkaline, or has an unclean or chlorinated taste. It is probably a good idea to secure distilled bottled water for your strike water in this scenario.

Remember the old saying, "garbage in, garbage out". Don't be surprised if the resulting beer tastes off if you start brewing with garbage tasting water.

4. Make A Large Wort Volume

Don't be afraid to go big, as this will improve your final product. Brewing a larger-volume extract batch will mitigate two common problems homebrewers often face.

Firstly, a large volume of wort will reduce the likelihood of your beer picking up an unintended darker colour. One common complaint among extract brewers is that their beer comes out darker than the style profile indicates. The simplest way to mitigate darkening is to increase your batch volume.

Secondly, many extract brewers face issues with hop utilisation. Wort with a lower specific gravity (more water than sugars) will help you utilise your hops more effectively and get the correct components out.

Generally, there is little reason not to maximise your wort volume with an extract batch. Ordering a 4- to 7-gallon brewing pot is a moderate expense. Many retailers sell high-quality 5-gallon pots for only $25 (£18). The only reason to brew a batch of fewer than 5 gallons is if your heat source cannot manage an even boil with anything larger. You may even consider boiling your wort in two smaller batches, concurrently or after another, and then combining them in your fermenter.

5. Add and Dissolve Malts Correctly

When brewing with malt extract, it's tempting to assume that all you need to do is pour in your extract, giving your wort the perfect colour, aroma, flavour profile, body, and strength. While it's true that your extract is essentially distilled wort that needs to be rehydrated in hot water, you still have to be smart about how you perform this infusion.

Firstly, you have to pour in your extract slowly and stir constantly. If you just pitch the whole container into boiling water, it will clump and burn, caramelising and darkening. This can give your wort and final beer a darker appearance and more burnt taste than you wanted.

A good rule of thumb is to kill the flame on your boiling strike water before adding malt extract. Stir until all the clumps and blobs are dissolved. Keep stirring for a few minutes, then turn the flame back on.

Remember, the longer you heat your wort, the darker and toastier it will get. Once dissolved in your water, malt extract only needs about fifteen minutes of heating to become thoroughly sterilised.

Move as quickly as you can to the hop boil, and only boil hops as long as your recipe requires. Having a dozen people queue up to smell the beautiful cannabinoid aromas from your hops can be a 'recipe for disaster' (literally), as you may over-boil your wort.

One final tip for effectively dissolving your extract: withhold some of it until late in the boil. This is an excellent way to ensure a more fresh, unburnt malt flavour. If you're working with 2.5-gallon concentrated wort, pour in half the malt at the end of the boil. If you're doing a 3.3-gallon concentrated wort, withhold one-third of the extract until the end.

6. Add Base and Speciality Malts

While DME and LME can adequately supply the flavour, colour, and fermentable sugars you need from base malt, they often fall short of imparting aroma. This is just part and parcel of the way malt extract is produced. Much of the malted grain scent is lost during the evaporation process.

A great way to recoup some of that cereal/caramel scent is to steep a certain amount of base malt, bearing in mind that this should be done at the beginning as a specific temperature is needed.

Some typical base malts you might want to add are:

- **Two-row malt** - Used across many styles
- **Pilsner malt** - Used in Pilsners and other light lagers, as well as many lighter ales
- **Pale malt** - Slightly darker than Pilsner malt. Used in Pale Ales, Brown Ales, Porters, and Stouts
- **Vienna malt** - A fully toasted malt, standard in Marzens and Ambers
- **Munich Malt** - This malt imparts toffee-like notes, common in darker German beers like Oktoberfests and Doppelbocks

When adding base malts in this fashion, you should subtract a certain amount of malt extract from the recipe. In a sense, you combine the extract with a bit of wort you made yourself with steeped grain.

The process goes like this:

1. For a 5-gallon extract batch, submerge 2.5 lbs (1.13 kg) of base malt into about 5 quarts (4.7 litres) of water, heated to 148–158 °F (64–70 °C).
2. Steep these grains for 45 minutes to one hour in a muslin bag.
3. Increase your strike water to the volume specified in your recipe
4. Add your malt extract, deducting 0.53 lbs (240 g) of DME or 0.73 lbs (331 g) of LME for each pound of milled base malt you steeped.

Alternatively, for speciality grains, you can submerge them in 1–3 quarts (0.95-2.8 litres) of strike water per pound (453 g) of grain. Steep them for the time stipulated by your recipe, then rinse the extracted bag with one half to one whole quart (or up to a litre) of water per pound of grain. The resulting liquid can be added to your wort.

This process is the most efficient way to draw out all the colours, scents, and flavours from your speciality grains without leeching undesirable tannins into the wort.

7. Exchange Some Extract for Sugar

Generally, dry and liquid malt extract is less fermentable than milled grain. Many homebrewers attempt to boost the quantity of fermentable sugars in their wort by increasing the amount of extract in the recipe. While this certainly will lead to a stronger beer, it will also darken the beer and thicken its mouthfeel, which may be undesirable.

One solution is to augment your malt extract—not with more malt extract, but with sugar. Unlike LME or DME, sugar is 100% fermentable. It increases the final alcohol content of your beer without altering the character.

In the past, adding standard sugar to homebrew was frowned upon. It was considered similar to using 'tasteless' rice and corn adjuncts, like those used by macro-brewers to make their cheap, fizzy lagers. Luckily, that stigma has since subsided. When employed judiciously, sugar infusions are now an acceptable solution to original gravity issues.

If you are looking to fine-tune your original gravity before fermentation, consider substituting a little extract for cane or corn sugar. You can replace your malt extract at the following ratios:

- For liquid malt, deduct 1 lb (454 g) of LME for every 13 oz (369 g) of sugar you add.
- For dry malt, deduct DME equal to the sugar you add. So, 1 oz of sugar added should be balanced with 1 oz of DME removed.

Just to note: don't go too crazy adding sugar. You should never remove more than 30% of your malt extract in exchange for sugar. Reducing your malt will result in the final beer lightening in colour. If your sugar addition exceeds 10%, you will also need to add 1/4 teaspoon of yeast nutrients to your wort.

Finally, having original gravity issues is essentially an all-grain brewer's problem. After conducting a mash yourself, you can never be 100% sure how much fermentable sugar your malted grain will produce. As you will discover in the next book, 'All-Grain Brewing Mastery', many variables will determine the quantity of fermentable sugars released from milled grain.

Almost everything is measured out for you in an extract brew, meaning you shouldn't have original gravity problems if you follow the recipe—but it's still possible! So you should always check and use the solutions above to correct if necessary.

8.Get the Most from your Hops

There are a few best practices concerning hop utilisation, some of which link with what has already been mentioned above.

Lower Your Overall Wort Density - Having a lower overall wort density improves hop utilisation, particularly with regard to bitterness. The bitterness in a beer is caused by the number of alpha acids (AA) released into the wort. A lower wort density will allow more of these alpha acids to be extracted during the boil.

Lose the Bag - There's no doubt that steeping bags make spent hops easier to fish out, but sadly, they also prevent some alpha acids from finding their way into your wort.

You can vastly improve your hops' bittering capabilities by throwing them in loose. During cooling, they will settle at the bottom of the brew pot along with your break material. You can easily siphon around this residue or run your wort through a sanitised stainless-steel strainer.

Bring in the Magnum - If you really want to maximise the bitterness of your homebrew, you might want to bring in the big dogs of the hop world. Magnum hops have a huge alpha acid content of approximately 16%. In contrast, they do lack flavour, unlike Centennial or Mosaic. You can consider them an excellent option for adding bitterness without gaining the additional citrus, resin, or spice that other bittering hops may bring.

9. Cool the Wort Correctly

It's far too easy to become complacent at the end of the boil and insufficiently cool down your wort. This is especially true when you are brewing a condensed extract batch and need to add water to dilute it in the fermenter.

Let's be crystal clear: even refrigerated water will not cool your hot wort sufficiently to pitch your yeast. Three gallons of 40°F (4°C) water poured over two gallons of boiled wort will not cool it below 110°F (43°C). This is well above any temperature where yeast can survive.

As time-consuming and laborious as it may be, you should cool your wort in the brewing pot/kettle before adding additional water or transferring it to your primary fermenter.

As with all types of brewing, you need to focus on preparation. If you don't own a wort chiller coil (as most novice homebrewers won't), you must think about how you will cool your pot or kettle before you begin on brew day. Hopefully, your kitchen sink is broad and deep enough to provide a decent cooling bath if you're using ice.

If the kitchen sink doesn't work, you could use a deeper utility 'slop' sink or your bathtub. Wherever you choose, just make sure you have a plan to transport the wort. A little sloshing right after brewing is not a big deal, but spilling an entire batch of wort on route to your bathtub surely is.

In addition, if you're using an ice bath to cool your brew pot/kettle, buy some large bags of ice. You will need a lot. You'll not be able to cool your wort with the three measly ice trays in your freezer.

Finally, if the bathtub is your only option, you must consider its size. Too much ice will be needed to fill an entire bathtub, so you may want to section it off to get ready for brew day. The best way to do this is using a bathtub divider made for babies (known as a 'BabyDam'). It will save you a little money compared to a brewer's wort chiller; however, if you don't want to spend the extra 55$ (£40), you may want to make one yourself using the idea as inspiration. If you're anything like me, seeing a chilling pot of wort in your bathtub instead of a baby is somewhat satisfying.

10. Pitch the Right Amount of Healthy Yeast

Among beermakers, a famous saying: "Brewers make wort; yeast makes beer."

All previous tips aim to provide your yeast with the best beer-making environment possible. Once you have brewed a wort with clean strike water, an adequate batch volume, plenty of fermentable sugars, and efficiently deployed hops, you need to make sure you have enough healthy yeast cells to turn it into beer.

Just like you thought ahead about the best way to cool your wort, you need to also prepare your yeast in advance. Ask yourself the following questions:

1. What is the pitching rate for my batch, and does my yeast product on hand satisfy it?
2. If not, what kind of yeast starter do I need?
3. If it does, does my yeast' smack pack' require additional prep time?

Brewer's Friend, the site recommended in chapter 6 on Priming, also has a handy yeast pitch rate calculator. It's especially beneficial since it asks you to enter your batch information and yeast product information. With this, the calculator advises you of your recipe's ideal pitching rate, the sufficiency of your current yeast supply, and what you must do to bring your yeast count to an appropriate level. It is obviously best to consult the calculator days before your plan to brew. A yeast starter takes several days to reach the correct number of cells, and you won't have time to do this 'on the fly' while your wort is cooling.

In the end, pitching an adequate, healthy, growing amount of yeast into your wort will lead to a fast and efficient fermentation process. Then you can expect a finished, potent, fully attenuated, and conditioned beer.

The previous tips can help you avoid some common pitfalls that novice homebrewers experience in their first extract batch. These include:

- Gushing bottles and rancid beer
- Off-smells and flavours
- Overly dark appearance
- Bland malt character
- Weak bitterness
- Slow or stalled fermentation

Beyond that, having this knowledge will help you fine-tune your extract beer. Whether that means bolstering its base malt aromas or adding an extra shot of bitterness with some Magnum hops, the end result will be tastier and even more satisfying.

Chapter Nine

Final Thoughts

The good ship beer is ready to hit the high seas.

I hope you enjoyed reading this book as much as I enjoyed writing it. I hope you found it to be entertaining, engaging, and informative. Armed with this information, you should now have all the tools necessary to take on your first malt extract beer recipe.

Before you embark on your first brew, I suggest you glance back briefly to Chapters 1 and 2, as these will help you secure everything you need for your inaugural batch. Starting with an extract recipe will slightly limit your ability to personalise your beer. Still, it will allow you to begin with a pre-packaged kit. Homebrew starter kits take a lot of the guesswork out of ingredient portions, brewing times, pitching rates, and priming measurements. Of course, after reading the next book, *All-Grain Brewing Mastery*, you will be able to do all of these things yourself with relatively little fuss.

While homebrew starter kits usually include most of the beer making equipment you need, I still advise reviewing the list of a la carte equipment given in Chapter 2. Ensuring that you have every item you need will save you a lot of headaches on brew day. You should also consider investing in more luxury items to make future batches easier to manage. A large brew pot and a good auto-siphon are the most important of these items. As you become more advanced, you may find yourself itching to buy more professional equipment, like a self-heating brew kettle, wort chilling coil, or a full beer kegging setup. At least you'll be able to buy a smaller wallet.

Remember that planning for your first brew day is about more than just making sure you have the right equipment. Several days before you plan to brew, you should confirm the yeast pitching rate and determine if you need a yeast starter. For a packaged kit, you most likely won't, but you do need to be 100% certain before you start steeping grain or boiling strike water.

The most important thing to ensure success with your first homebrew is to sanitise well. This is why I have dedicated the entirety of Chapter 3 to sanitising practices and also come back to the topic in nearly every subsequent chapter! Having a clear plan to clean and sterilise your equipment is imperative. Make time to heat-sanitise your metal and glass items and containers. Alternatively, you can secure a high-quality no-rinse sanitiser, like StarSan or PBW. Also, boil and cool any water you intend to add to your wort after flameout.

Once you start brewing, it's a great idea to have every ingredient and piece of equipment within reach. Open up your hop packets ahead of time. Have your steeping bags ready. Sanitise your primary fermenting bucket, lid, and airlock.

Have a plan to dispose of spent grains, brew pot sediment, and excess packaging. When it comes time to cool your wort and move it to your bucket for fermentation, the last thing you want is to slip on a bag of waterlogged malt you tossed on the floor in a blind panic! Looking over Chapter 4 before getting started will help guide you through the planning.

Once you have finished making your wort and pitching your yeast, you will need a dark, temperature-controlled space to store it. This is another aspect you need to plan for ahead of time. If your first extract beer is a lager, you will need to stow the fermenter in a spare refrigerator. A dark closet or basement pantry will work just fine if it's a middle-strength ale.

After you seal your fermenter and stow it away, I suggest referring to Chapter 5, which discusses the fermentation process. The section on specific gravity will be of particular importance at this point. Become familiar with your hydrometer and get ready to check your wort's gravity daily as fermentation enters its second week. Your homebrew kit instructions will likely indicate the length of time you should allow for fermentation, but the only way to ensure that your beer is fully fermented and attenuated is by taking hydrometer readings.

When you're confident that fermentation has concluded, it's time to prime and bottle. Chapter 6 will help you find the best priming sugar for your beer and give advice on adding it to the fermenter or bottling bucket. Subsequently, Chapter 7 takes you through the entire bottling process.

From here on out, it's all about waiting. Waiting is the hardest part of making your own beer. You'll twiddle your thumbs, watching your yeast starter burbling, your wort percolating, and your beer conditioning behind brown-tinted bottles. All of these stages will surely leave you burning with anticipation.

Undoubtedly, this same anticipation burned inside the ancient Mesopotamians, European monks, Bavarian lager-makers, Dublin Stout-makers, Brussels Lambic-makers, early craft beer pioneers in California, and countless other professional and novice brewers scattered across the globe.

Believe me, no beer is as satisfying as the first homebrewed beer you crack open. It's unique and memorable in a way no professionally-made beer can be. It's yours, from brew pot to glass.

Now that you have the physical and mental tools to make your own beer confidently, it's time to get cracking!

But before you go, I just want to ask you for a small but very important favour. Every author loves to see their book reviewed on Amazon. It helps us to sell more books and to refine future works. With this in mind, I would be deeply grateful for your feedback on *Beer Brewing Bliss: Extract Brewing Basics*. Also, please mention in your review what kind of beer you brewed after finishing this book. I can't wait to hear about the fantastic beer you brought into the world!

Acknowledgments

A huge thanks to the owners and contributors of the following sites, which have been used in support of the information given in this book.

1. www.bbcgoodfood.com
2. www.wikipedia.org
3. www.kegerator.com
4. www.homebrewacademy.com
5. www.howtohomebrewbeers.com
6. www.homebrewadvice.com
7. www.mrbeer.com
8. www.brewcabin.com
9. www.beerandbrewing.com
10. www.homebrewersassociation.org
11. www.sciencedirect.com

12. www.byo.com
13. www.freshops.com
14. www.howtobrew.com
15. www.beercraftr.com
16. www.winning-homebrew.com
17. www.beercreation.com
18. www.brewersfriend.com
19. www.northernbrewer.com
20. www.craftbeer.com
21. www.beerandwinejournal.com

Printed in Great Britain
by Amazon

23526526R00108